Gooseberry Patch®

W9-CEF-744

CHRISTMAS
In the Country

Family recipes, merry gifts from the kitchen and sweet holiday memories to celebrate the simple joys of the season.

A Country Store In Your Mailbox®

Gooseberry Patch
600 London Road
P.O. Box 190
Delaware, OH 43015

www.gooseberrypatch.com
1·800·854·6673

Copyright 2007, Gooseberry Patch 978-1-933494-23-4
Second Printing, August, 2007

Do you have a tried & true recipe...
tip, craft or memory that you'd like to see featured in a **Gooseberry
Patch** book? Visit our website at **www.gooseberrypatch.com**, register
and follow the easy steps to submit your favorite family recipe.
Or send them to us at:

Gooseberry Patch
Attn: Book Dept.
P.O. Box 190
Delaware, OH 43015

Don't forget to include the number of servings your recipe makes,
plus your name, address, phone number and e-mail address.
If we select your recipe, your name will appear right along with
it...and you'll receive a **FREE** copy of the book!

CONTENTS

DEDICATION

To everyone who loves the scent of
fresh-cut pine, the aroma of warm
gingerbread and going home for Christmas.

APPRECIATION

For our families, friends and
neighbors...wishing you the sweetest
of holiday memories.

Frosty
MORNINGS

Christmas Morning Stuffed Omelet

Weda Mosellie
Phillipsburg, NJ

*These omelets are easy to whip up while the kids
are playing with their gifts.*

8-oz. pkg. sliced mushrooms
1 onion, minced
6 T. butter, divided
8 eggs
1/4 c. milk
1 t. vanilla extract

1 t. all-purpose flour
salt and pepper to taste
8-oz. pkg. shredded mozzarella
  cheese
Optional: fresh chives, chopped

In a small skillet, sauté mushrooms and onion in 3 tablespoons butter until soft; set aside. Whisk together eggs, milk, vanilla, flour, salt and pepper in a bowl. Melt remaining butter in a large skillet; add egg mixture and cook for 5 to 8 minutes over low heat. Spoon mushroom mixture over one-half of eggs; sprinkle cheese over mushrooms. With a spatula, carefully flip other half of eggs onto cheese-topped half. Heat an additional 3 to 5 minutes over low heat, until cheese melts. Garnish with chives, if desired. Makes 2 to 4 servings.

Little extras for Christmas morning...a small wrapped gift at each place setting, soft holiday music in the background and no lights allowed except those on the tree. So magical!

Farmhouse Breakfast Bake

Vickie

*Wedges of this hearty farm-style breakfast are terrific served
with a frosty glass of orange juice.*

9-inch pie crust
1/2 lb. ground pork sausage,
  browned and drained
1 c. frozen diced potatoes,
  thawed
1/4 c. green onion, sliced
1/4 c. red or green pepper,
  chopped

1/2 c. shredded sharp Cheddar
  cheese, divided
4 eggs
1/4 c. milk
1/4 t. seasoned salt
1/4 t. pepper

Place pie crust in pie plate on baking sheet; sprinkle sausage in crust.
Top with potatoes, onion, red or green pepper and 1/4 cup cheese;
set aside. Beat together eggs, milk, seasoned salt and pepper; pour
over sausage mixture in crust. Bake for 30 minutes at 375 degrees,
or until egg mixture is set and crust is lightly golden. Sprinkle with
remaining cheese. Serves 6.

Keep tree trimming sweet & simple...little ones will love
helping out. Decorate your tree with paper chains,
homebaked cookies and dried apple or orange slices.

Holiday Morning French Toast

Coleen Lambert
Casco, WI

*A scrumptious breakfast treat that's sure to have family
& friends asking for the recipe.*

1 c. brown sugar, packed
1/2 c. butter, melted
1 T. cinnamon, divided
3 to 4 Granny Smith apples,
   cored, peeled and thinly
   sliced

1/2 c. raisins
1 loaf French or Italian bread,
   sliced 1-inch thick
8 to 9 eggs
2 c. milk
1 T. vanilla extract

Combine brown sugar, butter and one teaspoon cinnamon in a lightly
greased deep 13"x9" baking pan. Add apples and raisins; toss to coat
well. Spread apple mixture evenly over bottom of baking pan. Arrange
slices of bread on top; set aside. Blend together eggs, milk, vanilla and
remaining cinnamon until well mixed. Pour mixture over bread,
soaking bread completely. Cover and refrigerate for 4 to 24 hours.
Cover with aluminum foil; bake for 40 minutes at 375 degrees.
Uncover and bake an additional 5 minutes. Let stand for 5 minutes.
Serve warm. Makes 12 servings.

Jam jars topped with red
checked fabric squares
are oh-so cheery on
a breakfast table. Guests
can help themselves and,
if they're lucky, may even
find a jar tucked into
their stocking!

Johnson Family Flapjacks

Dot Johnson
Dearborn, MI

Kids love these topped with peanut butter & jelly!

1 c. all-purpose flour	1-1/3 c. buttermilk
1 T. sugar	1 egg
1/2 t. baking powder	2 T. oil
1/2 t. baking soda	Garnish: butter, pancake syrup
1/4 t. salt	

Mix together dry ingredients in a large bowl; set aside. In a small bowl, whisk together buttermilk, egg and oil; gradually stir into flour mixture with a large wooden spoon. Drop by 1/4 cupfuls onto a greased griddle over medium heat. Heat until done on one side; flip and heat on other side. Serve with butter and syrup. Serves 4.

Pour pancake batter into holiday-shaped cookie cutters. Trees, snowmen, wreaths and ornament shapes are all sweet. Remember to coat the inside of each cutter with non-stick vegetable spray and slip a clip-on style clothespin to the side for ease in turning the pancake.

Company Breakfast Casserole

*Nancy Molldrem
Eau Claire, WI*

This recipe is one I know I can count on for holiday breakfast buffets.

6-oz. pkg. seasoned croutons
1 lb. ground pork sausage,
   browned and drained
1 c. shredded Cheddar cheese
8 eggs

3 c. milk
1/2 t. dry mustard
1/2 t. salt
2 c. corn flake cereal, crushed
1/2 c. butter, melted

Place croutons in the bottom of a lightly greased 13"x9" baking pan; top with sausage. Sprinkle with cheese; set aside. Beat eggs, milk, mustard and salt together; pour over cheese. Cover; refrigerate overnight. Before baking, top with cereal; drizzle with butter. Bake at 350 degrees for 45 minutes; cool for 10 minutes. Serves 6 to 8.

Sugar Plum Breakfast

*Sharon Kochan
Overland Park, KS*

So easy to whip up!

4 eggs, beaten
1 t. vanilla extract
1/3 c. sugar

2/3 c. all-purpose flour
2 c. milk
1/4 c. butter, melted

Beat eggs, vanilla, sugar, flour and milk together; set aside. Pour butter in a 13"x9" pan; spoon egg mixture over the top. Bake at 425 degrees for 30 minutes. Serves 4.

Christmas Eve, after I had hung my stocking, I lay awake a long time, pretending to be asleep and keeping alert to see what Santa Claus would do when he came.

-Hellen Keller

Ham & Cheddar Quiche

Cheri Emery
Quincy, IL

Quiche is a great dish to pop in the oven to bake while stockings and gifts are being opened.

9-inch pie crust	1/2 pt. half-and-half
1 c. cooked ham, diced	1 t. onion powder
1 c. shredded Cheddar cheese	1/2 t. salt
2 eggs	1/8 t. pepper

Line unbaked pie crust with aluminum foil; bake at 400 degrees for 5 minutes. Remove aluminum foil; bake an additional 5 minutes. Arrange ham and cheese in crust; set aside. Whisk together eggs, half-and-half, onion powder, salt and pepper; pour over cheese. Cover edges of pie crust with aluminum foil. Bake at 400 degrees for 35 to 40 minutes, until a knife inserted near the center comes out clean. Let stand for 5 to 10 minutes; cut into wedges. Serves 6.

Place setting ornaments are surprisingly simple to make! Gather up mittens, blanket stitch a felt star cut-out to the front, fill with goodies and add a loop of wire for hanging on a chair back.

Southern Cornmeal Pancakes

Teresa Stiegelmeyer
Indianapolis, IN

My mother, being from the South, often made these
quick & easy pancakes.

3/4 c. yellow cornmeal	1/2 t. salt
1/4 c. all-purpose flour	3/4 c. milk
1-1/2 t. baking powder	2 T. oil

Combine cornmeal, flour, baking powder and salt; stir in milk and oil.
Pour by 1/4 cupfuls of batter onto a hot greased griddle; cook until
both sides are golden. Makes 6.

Country Sausage & Apples

Donna Maltman
Toledo, OH

A truly delicious, old-fashioned favorite recipe.

1-lb. pkg. smoked sausage,	1 c. brown sugar, packed
sliced into 1-inch pieces	1/4 to 1/2 c. water
3 Granny Smith apples, cored	
and diced	

Arrange sausage in a slow cooker; top with apples. Sprinkle with
brown sugar; pour water over the sugar. Stir gently; cover and cook on
high setting for 1-1/2 to 2 hours. Makes 4 servings.

For a sparkling twist on the traditional paper chain, use only
silver and white paper. Hang chains over your breakfast table,
around the doorway or along the mantel.

Pennsylvania Dutch Scrapple

Virginia Watson
Scranton, PA

Squares of this savory dish are traditionally served at breakfast.

1 lb. boneless pork loin, chopped
1 c. cornmeal
14-1/2 oz. can chicken broth
1/4 t. dried thyme
1/4 t. salt

1/2 c. all-purpose flour
1/4 t. pepper
2 T. oil
Garnish: pancake syrup

Cover pork with water; bring to a boil over medium heat. Simmer until fork tender, about an hour. Drain and place in a food processor; process until finely minced. Combine pork, cornmeal, broth, thyme and salt in a large saucepan over medium heat; bring to a boil. Reduce heat and simmer for 2 minutes, or until mixture is very thick, stirring constantly. Line a 9"x5" loaf pan with wax paper, letting paper extend 3 to 4 inches above top of pan. Spoon pork mixture into pan; cover and chill in refrigerator for 4 hours or overnight. Unmold; cut into squares and set aside. Combine flour and pepper; sprinkle squares with flour mixture. Heat oil over medium heat in a large skillet; cook on both sides until golden. Serve with syrup. Serves 12.

Whip up place markers in no time. Secure stickers along the outer edges of simple construction paper shapes and write the name inside. Punch a hole in each and slip a holiday florist's pick through.

Cranberry Swirl Coffee Cake

Evelyn Love
Standish, ME

This recipe is a long-time favorite I enjoy with
a glass of ice-cold milk.

1/2 c. margarine, softened
1 c. sugar
2 eggs, beaten
2 c. all-purpose flour
1 t. baking powder
1 t. baking soda
1/2 t. salt

8-oz. container sour cream
1 t. almond extract
1/2 t. vanilla extract
16-oz. can whole-berry
   cranberry sauce, divided
1/2 c. chopped nuts

Mix together margarine and sugar until smooth. Add eggs, one at a time; set aside. Combine flour, baking powder, baking soda and salt in a large bowl. Add to margarine mixture, alternating with sour cream. Stir in extracts; mix well. Pour half the batter into a greased 8" tube pan; add half the cranberry sauce and swirl around with a knife. Add remaining batter; top with remaining cranberry sauce, swirling around with a knife. Sprinkle with nuts. Bake at 350 degrees for 50 minutes; cool for 5 minutes. Remove to rack; drizzle with topping. Serves 16.

Topping:

3/4 c. powdered sugar
1/2 t. almond extract

1 to 3 T. warm water

Combine powdered sugar and extract; add water one tablespoon at a time to make it a drizzling consistency.

Christmas...is not an eternal event at all,
but a piece of one's home that one carries in one's heart.

-Freya Stark

Gingerbread Scones

Cassandra Skaggs
Castaic, CA

Scones that are so easy to make and taste
wonderful every time!

2 c. all-purpose flour
3 T. brown sugar, packed
2 t. baking powder
1/2 t. baking soda
1/2 t. salt
1 t. ground ginger
1/2 t. ground cloves
1/2 t. allspice
1/2 t. cinnamon
1/4 c. butter
1/3 c. molasses
1 egg yolk, beaten
1/4 c. milk
Garnish: sugar, nutmeg

Combine flour, brown sugar, baking powder, baking soda, salt and spices in a mixing bowl. Cut in butter with a pastry blender until mixture resembles coarse crumbs. Make a well in the center; set aside. In a small mixing bowl, stir together molasses, egg yolk and milk. Add all at once to well in flour mixture; stir with fork until combined. Knead dough on a lightly floured surface for 10 to 12 strokes, until nearly smooth. Pat dough into an 8-inch circle; cut into 8 wedges. Sprinkle with sugar and nutmeg. Arrange on an ungreased baking sheet. Bake for 12 to 15 minutes at 400 degrees. Let cool on wire rack for 20 minutes. Makes 8.

Place a paper cut-out snowflake between 2 clear glass plates...
what a magical way to begin the day!

Overnight Buttermilk-Raisin Pancakes

Bev Ray
Brandon, FL

These pancakes are a breakfast time-saver, so we can enjoy every minute of Christmas morning.

2 c. quick-cooking oats,
   uncooked
2 c. buttermilk
1/2 c. all-purpose flour
2 T. sugar
1 t. baking powder

1 t. baking soda
1/2 t. cinnamon
1/2 t. salt
2 eggs, beaten
1/4 c. butter, softened
1/3 c. raisins

Mix together oats and buttermilk in a medium bowl; cover and refrigerate overnight. In a large bowl, sift together flour, sugar, baking powder, baking soda, cinnamon and salt. Make a well in the center; add oat mixture, eggs, butter and raisins. Stir just until moistened. Allow batter to stand for 20 minutes before cooking. If batter is too thick, add buttermilk one tablespoon at a time, until batter reaches desired consistency. Heat a lightly greased large skillet over medium heat. Pour batter by 1/4 cupfuls onto skillet. Cook pancakes until bubbles appear on top; flip and cook until golden. Serves 9.

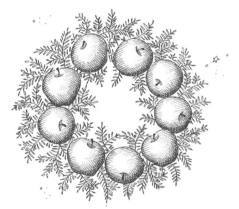

Deck the front door with a little unexpected color...instead of red apples, secure bright green Granny Smith apples to a traditional greenery wreath.

Slow-Cooker Hashbrown Casserole
Jessica Robertson
Fishers, IN

*Sometimes I'll substitute bacon or ham in
place of the sausage.*

32-oz. pkg. frozen shredded
   hashbrowns
1 lb. ground pork sausage,
   browned and drained
1 onion, diced
1 green pepper, diced

1-1/2 c. shredded Cheddar
   cheese
1 doz. eggs
1 c. milk
1 t. salt
1 t. pepper

Place one-third each of hashbrowns, sausage, onion, green pepper and cheese in a lightly greased slow cooker. Repeat layering 2 more times, ending with cheese. Beat eggs, milk, salt and pepper together in a large bowl; pour over top. Cover and cook on low setting for 10 hours. Serves 8.

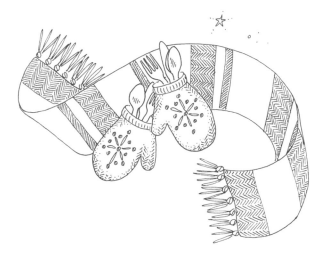

Slip silverware into woolly gloves, mittens or even a cap when
setting the breakfast table. Add a knitted scarf to create
a whimsical table runner!

Slow-Cooker Apple Oatmeal

Dana Thompson
Gooseberry Patch

Make this, and you'll love the aroma you wake up to!

2 c. milk
1/4 c. brown sugar, packed
1 T. butter, melted
1/4 t. salt
1/2 t. cinnamon
1 c. quick-cooking oats,
   uncooked

1 c. apple, cored, peeled and
   finely chopped
1/2 c. raisins or chopped dates
1/2 c. chopped walnuts or
   almonds

Combine all ingredients in a greased slow cooker; mix well. Cover and cook on low setting for 8 to 9 hours or overnight. Stir before serving. Serves 6 to 8.

Grandma's china and Mom's silver...if not now, when will you use them? Make the holiday even more special by dressing up your table with sentimental, handed-down favorites.

Nutty Cherry Oatmeal

Annette Ingram
Grand Rapids, MI

A warm and filling breakfast for those frosty mornings.

2-1/2 c. water
1-1/2 c. long-cooking oats,
    uncooked
1/2 t. cinnamon

1/4 c. sweetened, dried cherries
1/4 c. chopped pecans
Garnish: brown sugar, milk

In a large saucepan, bring water to boil over high heat. Add oats and return to a boil. Cook and stir constantly for one minute; reduce heat. Cover and simmer for 5 minutes, or until water is absorbed, stirring once or twice. Stir in cinnamon, cherries and pecans. Top with brown sugar and milk. Serves 6 to 8.

Unexpected tabletop decorations create frosty fun! Nestle taper candles in a tall vase and surround with artificial snow. Top empty juice glasses with jaunty Santa hats or top off a candlestick with a vintage ornament.

Apple Crunch Coffee Cake

Jill Carr
Sutter Creek, CA

This coffee cake stays so moist, you can even make it the night before.

1/3 c. butter, softened
1/3 c. shortening
2 c. sugar
2 eggs
3 c. all-purpose flour
2 t. baking powder

1/2 t. baking soda
1/4 t. salt
1 t. cinnamon
1-3/4 c. buttermilk
2 to 3 apples, cored, peeled
  and sliced

Beat together butter, shortening and sugar in a large bowl until light and fluffy. Add eggs, one at a time, beating well after each addition; set aside. Stir together flour, baking powder, baking soda, salt and cinnamon; add to butter mixture alternately with buttermilk. Spread half the batter into a greased 13"x9" baking pan; top with apples. Spread remaining batter over top of apples; sprinkle with topping. Bake at 350 degrees for 55 to 60 minutes, or until toothpick tests clean. Serves 12.

Topping:

1 c. all-purpose flour
1 c. brown sugar, packed

1 T. cinnamon
6 T. butter

Stir together flour, brown sugar and cinnamon. Cut in butter with a pastry blender until crumbly.

Sing hey! Sing hey! For Christmas Day;
twine mistletoe and holly.
For friendship glows in winter snows,
and so let's all be jolly!

-Traditional English Rhyme

Texas-Style Sausage Muffins

Kay Lowe
Tomball, TX

Muffins packed with flavor and just a kick of cayenne.

1/2 lb. ground pork sausage
1/3 c. green onion, chopped
1-1/2 c. biscuit baking mix
1-1/2 t. brown sugar, packed
1/2 t. dry mustard

1/4 t. cayenne pepper
2/3 c. milk
1/2 c. shredded Cheddar cheese

Cook and stir sausage and onion in a skillet until browned; drain on paper towels and set aside. Mix together biscuit mix, brown sugar, mustard and cayenne pepper in a medium bowl. Stir in sausage mixture, milk and cheese until just blended. Fill 12 greased muffin cups 2/3 full. Bake at 375 degrees for 20 to 25 minutes, until golden. Makes one dozen.

Jumbo Quiche Muffins

Debra Alf
Robbinsdale, MN

These oversized muffins are always a breakfast hit.

16.3-oz. tube refrigerated flaky
   buttermilk biscuits
1/2 c. cream cheese, softened
   and divided
4 eggs, beaten

1/4 t. seasoned salt
1/4 t. pepper
6 slices bacon, crisply cooked
   and crumbled
1/2 c. shredded Cheddar cheese

Place each biscuit into a greased jumbo muffin cup; press to form a well. Combine cream cheese, eggs, salt and pepper. Spoon 2 tablespoons egg mixture into each biscuit well; sprinkle with bacon and top with cheese. Bake at 375 degrees for 15 minutes. Serves 10.

Italian Doughnuts

Wendy Lee Paffenroth
Pine Island, NY

Easy to make, these doughnuts will disappear quickly!

16-oz. container ricotta cheese
2 c. all-purpose flour
5 eggs, beaten
5 T. sugar

4 t. baking powder
1 t. vanilla extract
2 c. oil
Garnish: powdered sugar

Mix together all ingredients except oil and powdered sugar in a large bowl. Mix well with a wooden spoon; set aside. Heat oil to 375 degrees in a heavy deep saucepan. Carefully drop dough by teaspoonfuls into hot oil. Cook until golden, 3 to 4 minutes; drain on paper towels. Place powdered sugar in a brown paper bag; add doughnuts a few at a time and shake to coat. Makes 5 dozen.

Sugared fruit sparkles when paired with tea lights as a holiday centerpiece. Brush whole fruit with corn syrup, then roll in coarse sugar. Arrange on a tiered stand with tealights.

Grandma Virginia's Doughnuts

Jean Livingood
Detroit Lakes, MN

Grandma Virginia has taught all of her granddaughters to make doughnuts. There was never a time when they came to visit that she didn't send a bag of doughnuts home with the kids.

2 c. buttermilk	1 t. baking soda
2 eggs, beaten	1/2 t. nutmeg
3 T. oil	1/4 t. salt
1/2 t. vanilla extract	4 c. all-purpose flour
1-1/2 c. sugar	1/2 c. oil

Mix together buttermilk, eggs, oil, and vanilla; set aside. In a large bowl, combine remaining ingredients except oil; stir into buttermilk mixture. Heat oil to 375 degrees in a deep saucepan. Drop batter into hot oil with a doughnut dropper, or by tablespoonfuls to make doughnut holes. Turn over when golden. Cool on paper towels. Makes 6 dozen.

For a lighthearted welcome, fill fanciful rubber or cowboy boots
with fresh greenery and sprigs of holly!

Gingerbread Pancakes

Kendall Hale
Lynn, MA

Oh-so scrumptious topped with tangy Lemon Sauce.

1-1/2 c. all-purpose flour	1/2 t. ground ginger
1 t. baking powder	1 egg
1/4 t. baking soda	1-1/4 c. milk
1/4 t. salt	1/4 c. molasses
1 t. cinnamon	3 T. oil

Sift together first 6 ingredients in a medium bowl; set aside. In a large bowl, beat egg and milk until well blended; stir in molasses and oil. Add flour mixture to milk mixture, stirring just until moistened. Pour batter by 1/2 cupfuls onto a lightly greased hot griddle. Cook over medium heat until bubbly on top; flip and continue to cook until golden. Serve with Lemon Sauce. Serves 4.

Lemon Sauce:

1/2 c. sugar	2 T. butter
1 T. cornstarch	1/2 t. lemon zest
1/8 t. nutmeg	2 T. lemon juice
1 c. water	

Stir together sugar, cornstarch and nutmeg in a small saucepan; add water. Cook over medium heat until thick and bubbly; cook and stir for an additional 2 minutes. Remove from heat; add remaining ingredients. Stir just until butter melts. Serve warm.

A jar of Lemon Sauce is a thoughtful gift for a letter carrier, school bus driver or teacher. Paired with a favorite pancake or waffle mix, they'll make for a very merry morning!

Mother's Honey Butter

Betty Romig
Smithton, MO

*I remember my father going to get honey from a bee tree when
I was small. Mother would use the honey in lots of recipes,
but this recipe was the one that my brothers and I loved most.*

1 c. honey
1 c. margarine, softened
1/2 t. cinnamon

1-1/2 to 2 c. powdered sugar
5 1/2-pint canning jars and lids,
   sterilized

Combine all ingredients in a mixing bowl. Mix with an electric mixer
on medium speed until powdered sugar is all mixed in and any lumps
are gone. Spoon into jars; store in refrigerator. Makes 5 jars.

Country Cabin Pancake Syrup

Rita Morgan
Pueblo, CO

*Slip a jar of syrup into a Christmas stocking along with
a pancake mix…a welcome surprise for neighbors.*

2 16-oz. pkgs. dark brown
   sugar
1 c. sugar
1/2 t. salt

4 c. water
3/4 c. corn syrup
1 T. maple extract

Combine all ingredients except maple extract in a saucepan. Bring to
a boil; boil for about 10 minutes, stirring constantly, until mixture is
thickened. Let cool to lukewarm; stir in extract. Refrigerate up to
4 weeks. Makes about 7 cups.

For a candle with whimsy, simply
fill a regular, quart-size Mason jar
with peppermint candies or gumdrops.
Insert an oyster jar votive holder inside
the rim and add a votive candle to
the holder...oh-so simple!

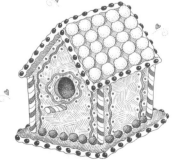

Buttermilk Cinnamon Rolls

Dobie Hill
Lubbock, TX

Light and tender cinnamon rolls...just like you remember.

3 c. all-purpose flour
4 t. baking powder
1/4 t. baking soda
1 t. salt
1/2 c. shortening

1-1/2 c. buttermilk
1/2 c. margarine, softened
1/2 c. sugar
1/2 t. cinnamon

Combine first 4 ingredients; cut in shortening until crumbs form. Stir in buttermilk until well blended; knead dough on a lightly floured surface for 4 to 5 minutes. Roll out to 1/4-inch thickness; spread margarine over dough to edges. In a small bowl, mix sugar and cinnamon; sprinkle over dough. Roll up jelly-roll style; cut into 1/2-inch slices. Place on a greased baking sheet; bake at 450 degrees for 10 to 12 minutes. Makes about one dozen.

Pull out vintage finds when setting a buffet table. An old door hinge becomes a clever napkin holder when a sprig of greenery is tied on. Its weight keeps napkins in their place...how clever!

Auntie Ruth's Potatoes

Dana Cunningham
Lafayette, LA

Always a breakfast "must-have" when family visits for the holidays.

2 slices bacon, crisply cooked, crumbled and drippings reserved
2 T. butter
4 potatoes, peeled and thinly sliced
1 T. onion, diced
2 eggs
salt and pepper to taste
1/2 c. shredded Cheddar cheese

Melt butter with reserved drippings in skillet. Add potatoes and onion; cover and cook over medium heat, stirring occasionally, until potatoes are golden and tender. Reduce heat; crack eggs over potatoes and stir gently. Sprinkle with salt, pepper, cheese and reserved bacon. Cook over low heat until eggs are firm and cheese melts. Serves 4.

Light up the morning! Tuck a votive in a clear glass mug, surround with coffee beans and tuck in a mini candy cane. Tie on a ribbon and march several right down the center of the breakfast table.

In the Nick of Time...
theme gift ideas you can put together in a snap!

Baker's Delight...line a vintage-style mixing bowl with a tea towel and arrange layered cookie and brownie mixes, measuring cups and spoons, a spatula, wooden spoon and several of your favorite recipes.

Family Night...fill a gift bag with a puzzle, board game, bags of microwave popcorn, snack mixes, holiday videos and frosty sodas.

Ice Cream Lover...tuck sundae dishes, an ice cream scoop, chocolate, caramel and strawberry ice cream toppings, maraschino cherries and nuts into a basket.

Soup's On...add soup mugs, layered soup mixes, cornbread and hot roll mixes, crackers, butter and soup spoons to a bean pot or enamelware stockpot.

Best-Ever Sausage & Spinach Dip

Jane Gavarkavich
Martins Ferry, OH

Vary the flavor of this delicious dip by using different types of sausage. Sweet Italian sausage gives the dip a mild flavor, while zesty chicken sausage will taste spicy, but is lower in fat.

1 T. oil
12-oz. pkg. ground hot
    pork sausage
1 onion, minced
1 clove garlic, minced

8-oz. pkg. cream cheese, cubed
16-oz. jar salsa
10-oz. pkg. frozen chopped
    spinach, thawed and drained

Place oil, sausage, onion and garlic in a large skillet. Cook, breaking up sausage, until sausage is browned and onion is golden; drain. Stir in remaining ingredients; simmer gently for about 5 minutes, until heated through and cream cheese is melted. Serve hot. Makes about 7-1/2 cups.

An icy luminaria...so simple! Set a paper cup filled with rocks inside a clean, empty ice cream tub. Surround the cup with cranberries and greenery, then add water to just below the cup rim. Freeze until solid, remove the cup, peel away the ice cream tub and slip in a votive.

WELCOME
Friends

Fabulous 4-Cheese Spread

Francie Stutzman
Dalton, OH

For me, this is the absolute best spread for crackers!
A sure-fire hit for holiday open houses and office parties.

12-oz. pkg. shredded sharp
   Cheddar cheese
1/2 c. cream cheese, softened
4-oz. pkg. crumbled blue cheese
1/2 c. mayonnaise

1/4 c. grated Parmesan cheese
2 T. onion, grated
1/8 t. hot pepper sauce
salt and pepper to taste

Combine all ingredients in a food processor; process until smooth.
Refrigerate. Makes about 1-1/2 cups.

Shortbread cookies tied with festive ribbon will look oh-so pretty
hanging in kitchen windowpanes.

Holiday Ham Balls

Jeanette Lawrence
Vacaville, CA

A family favorite for years. Good for breakfast too...mix ingredients up the night before and they'll be ready to bake when you get up.

3 c. biscuit baking mix
1-1/2 c. smoked ham, finely
   chopped
16-oz. pkg. shredded Cheddar
   cheese

2/3 c. milk
1/2 c. grated Parmesan cheese
2 T. dried parsley
2 t. spicy mustard

Mix all ingredients thoroughly; shape into one-inch balls. Place about 2 inches apart on a lightly greased 15"x10" jelly-roll pan. Bake at 350 degrees for 20 to 25 minutes, until lightly golden. Immediately remove from pan; serve warm. Makes 7 dozen.

Enjoy a springtime bouquet during winter's frosty days!
Fill a galvanized pail with pebbles, then tuck in a variety
of tulip, daffodil or hyacinth bulbs. Add just enough water to barely
cover the pebbles, keep watered, and in a few weeks you'll
have lots of springtime blossoms.

Loaded Potato Rounds

Claudine King
Fremont, MI

An amazing combination of flavors...you'll love these!

2 baking potatoes
olive oil
1 c. shredded Colby Jack cheese
6 slices bacon, crisply cooked
   and crumbled

1/3 c. green onion, sliced
1/4 c. barbecue sauce

Slice unpeeled potatoes into 1/4-inch thick rounds. Spray or brush with oil on both sides; arrange on an ungreased baking sheet. Bake at 450 degrees for 20 minutes, or until tender and golden. Mix together cheese, bacon and onion in a small bowl; set aside. Brush baked potato rounds with barbecue sauce; sprinkle with cheese mixture. Return to baking sheet; bake an additional 3 to 5 minutes, until cheese is melted. Makes 2-1/2 dozen.

Oh, the snow, the beautiful snow, Filling the sky and earth below,
Over the housetops, over the street,
Over the heads of people you meet;
Dancing—Flirting—Skimming along
Beautiful snow!

-J. W. Watson

Celebration Snack Mix

Helen Woodard
Necedah, WI

The ideal snack for munching on while enjoying all those classic Christmas movies!

4 c. bite-size crispy corn cereal
   squares
4 c. bite-size crispy rice cereal
   squares
1 c. dry-roasted peanuts
1 c. mini pretzels
1 t. sugar
2 t. paprika

1/2 t. garlic salt
1/2 t. onion powder
1/4 t. dry mustard
1/8 t. Cajun seasoning
3 T. oil
1-1/2 t. Worcestershire sauce
1/2 t. smoke-flavored cooking
   sauce

Place cereal, peanuts and pretzels in a 2-gallon plastic zipping bag; set aside. Mix together sugar and spices; set aside. Combine oil and sauces; mix well and pour over cereal mixture. Close bag; toss gently until well-coated. Add spice mixture a little at a time, close bag and toss until well-coated. Store in an airtight container. Makes about 8 cups.

Use vintage canning jars to share snack mixes with friends & neighbors. Tie on a bow and a tag and you're all set...what could be easier?

WELCOME
Friends

Cranberry-Orange Snack Mix

Mary Ann Nemecek
Springfield, IL

Teachers will love jars of this very merry mix!

2 c. bite-size crispy oat cereal
   squares
2 c. bite-size crispy corn cereal
   squares
2 c. mini pretzels
1 c. whole almonds
1/4 c. butter, melted
1/3 c. frozen orange juice
   concentrate, thawed

3 T. brown sugar, packed
1 t. cinnamon
3/4 t. ground ginger
1/4 t. nutmeg
2/3 c. sweetened, dried
   cranberries

Combine cereals, pretzels and almonds in a large bowl; set aside. Stir together melted butter, orange juice, brown sugar and spices until blended. Pour over cereal mixture; stir well to coat. Spread in a 13"x9" baking pan sprayed with non-stick vegetable spray. Bake at 250 degrees for 50 minutes, stirring every 10 minutes. Remove from oven and stir in cranberries. Place baking pan on a wire rack; let cool until mixture is crisp. Store in airtight containers. Makes about 8 cups.

Fill a bowl with buttons and nestle a pillar candle inside...so simple, but such a sweet decoration.

Christmas Snow Punch

Connie Herek
Bay City, MI

Children especially love the "snow" on top!

1-ltr. bottle red fruit punch, chilled
2-ltr. bottle lemon-lime soda, chilled

1/2 gal. vanilla ice cream

Stir together punch and soda in a punch bowl. Scoop ice cream in round balls like snowballs and float on top. Serves 15 to 20.

A gingerbread votive holder! Roll a gingerbread dough recipe
1/8-inch thick and cut in a 3"x9" rectangle. Lightly coat the outside
of an empty soda can with non-stick vegetable spray, wrap with
a dough rectangle, then wrap tightly with aluminum foil.
Lay can, seam-side down, in a 375-degree oven for 8 minutes.
Cool 5 minutes, remove foil and cool 3 minutes more.
Gently remove can, cool until hard, or set.

WELCOME
Friends

Golden Wassail

Emily Young
Edmond, OK

*Cups of this orange-cinnamon wassail
are sure to warm you up head-to-toe.*

4 c. unsweetened pineapple juice
4 c. apple cider
12-oz. can apricot nectar
1 c. orange juice

1/2 t. cardamom
2 4-inch cinnamon sticks
1 t. whole cloves
1/4 t. salt

Pour juices into a 20-cup coffee maker urn; place remaining ingredients in basket of urn. Allow to go through perk cycle of coffee maker. Strain; discard whole spices. Serve hot. Makes 20 servings.

It's as much fun as you remember...come on,
make snow angels!

Smokey Cheese Balls

Terry Zaccuri
Aliso Viejo, CA

*I freeze one of these delicious cheese balls, and then the next time
I have a party, my appetizer is already prepared!*

2 8-oz. pkgs. cream cheese,
   softened
2 c. smoked Fontina cheese,
   shredded and softened

1/2 c. butter, softened
2 T. milk
2 t. steak sauce
1 c. pecans, finely chopped

Blend together cheeses and butter. Add milk and steak sauce; beat until
fluffy. Cover and chill at least 4 hours or up to 24 hours. Shape into
2 balls; roll in pecans. Makes about 4-1/2 cups.

For a crisp holiday scent, hollow out grapefruit and orange
halves. Tuck a votive in the center of each and
surround the votives with fresh cranberries.

Cheesy Sausage Bread

Sharon Dennison
Floyds Knobs, IN

Try using Colby or Cheddar instead of Swiss in this recipe.

16-oz. pkg. hot roll mix
1-1/2 lbs. ground pork sausage
1 onion, chopped
1/2 c. Swiss cheese, grated
2 eggs, beaten

1/2 t. hot pepper sauce
2 T. dried parsley
1/4 c. grated Parmesan cheese
1/2 t. salt
Optional: butter

Prepare hot roll mix dough according to package directions. Let rise for 45 minutes; punch down and set aside. Brown together sausage and onion; drain. Combine sausage mixture with remaining ingredients except butter; let cool. Roll out dough on a floured surface into a 12"x8" rectangle; place on a lightly greased baking sheet. Spoon sausage mixture in center of dough. Fold long edges of rectangle over each other toward center of dough to cover sausage mixture, crimping together edges and ends. Bake at 400 degrees for 20 minutes, until golden. Butter may be spread over top in last few minutes of baking, if desired. Serves 6 to 8.

Hang stockings on
the backs of chairs,
doorknobs or
bedposts...
just for fun!

Over-Stuffed Mushrooms

Ruth Astor
Hodgenville, KY

*This recipe came from a 30-year-old cookbook from my husband's
church...always a family favorite. To make sure the onions are tender,
I sauté them in a little olive oil before adding to the filling mixture.*

1 lb. mushrooms
3 T. grated Parmesan cheese
1 clove garlic, pressed
1 onion, finely chopped
1 c. bread crumbs

1 T. fresh parsley, minced
2 T. butter, melted
salt and pepper to taste
6 T. oil, divided

Remove stems from mushrooms; set aside. Mix all remaining ingredients except oil; spoon into mushroom caps. Spread 2 tablespoons oil in
a 13"x9" baking pan; arrange mushrooms in pan. Drizzle remaining oil
equally over mushrooms; bake at 350 degrees for 20 minutes. Serves
4 to 6.

Olive Cheese Puffs

Tori Willis
Champaign, IL

With only 5 ingredients, this is a super recipe you have to try!

8-oz. pkg. shredded sharp
   Cheddar cheese
1/2 c. butter

1 c. all-purpose flour
1/8 t. cayenne pepper
48 green olives with pimentos

Blend cheese and butter together in a food processor; process until
smooth. Add flour and cayenne; mix well. Roll dough out on a lightly
floured surface to 1/4-inch thick; cut into 2-inch squares. Wrap
each square around an olive; press seams together to seal. Bake at
400 degrees on parchment paper-lined baking sheets for 10 to
15 minutes. Makes 4 dozen.

Be an elf...leave surprises on the doorsteps
of friends & neighbors!

WELCOME
Friends

Italian Cheese Sticks

Elaine Nichols
Mesa, AZ

String cheese never tasted so good!

12 1-oz. pkgs. string cheese
2 eggs
1 c. Italian-seasoned dry bread
    crumbs

Optional: pizza sauce

Unwrap cheese sticks; set aside. Beat eggs in a shallow bowl; place bread crumbs in a separate dish. Dip each cheese stick into egg, then into crumbs, then into egg again and into crumbs again. Arrange on a greased baking sheet. Chill at least 2 hours or freeze for about an hour. Bake at 400 degrees for 7 to 9 minutes. Serve warm with warmed pizza sauce for dipping, if desired. Makes one dozen.

This is meeting time again. Home is the magnet...doors thrown open, running shadows on snow, open arms, kisses, voices and laughter. All that is dear, that is lasting, renews its hold on us: we are home again.

-Elizabeth Bowen

Sweet Mustard Dip

Kim Smith
Greensburg, PA

This dip is wonderful with pretzels and crackers. It's also great on grilled chicken, ham, burgers or even as a dip for chicken fingers.

8-oz. jar spicy brown mustard
14-oz. can sweetened condensed
  milk

1 T. Worcestershire sauce
1 T. prepared horseradish

Blend all ingredients together; amount of horseradish can be adjusted to taste. Store in refrigerator. Makes about 2-1/2 cups.

Mexicali Bean Dip

Rhonda Merritt
Wayne, WV

So easy to whip up when friends drop by.

8-oz. pkg. cream cheese,
  softened
15-oz. can chili with beans

1 c. salsa
1 c. shredded Cheddar cheese

Spread cream cheese in the bottom of a 9" pie plate; set aside. Mix chili and salsa together; pour over cream cheese. Sprinkle with Cheddar cheese; bake at 350 degrees for 20 minutes. Serves 6 to 8.

Keep all of your family's favorite holiday story books in a basket by a cozy chair. Set aside one night as family night to read your favorites together.

Mom's Party Rye Spread

Jan Purnell
Littleston, PA

*When I was growing up, Mom made this appetizer every
Christmas Eve...there were never any leftovers!*

1/2 lb. bacon, chopped
8-oz. pkg. sharp Cheddar
   cheese, cubed
1 onion, chopped

1 t. Worcestershire sauce
salt to taste
16-oz. loaf sliced party rye

Combine all ingredients except party rye. Place in a food processor
and process into a paste consistency. Chill to combine flavors. To serve,
warm mixture slightly at room temperature to spreading consistency.
Spread on party rye slices; arrange on an ungreased baking sheet.
Place under a heated broiler until bacon is cooked and spread is golden,
about 3 to 5 minutes. Serve warm. Makes 4 dozen.

Share flower seeds from summer's garden with a far-away friend.
She'll love having some of your flowers pop up in her garden next
spring. What a thoughtful way to begin a friendship garden.

Cinnamon-Sugar Nuts

Kerry McNeil
Anacortes, WA

This is a favorite snack Mom made every Christmas while I was growing up. She lost the recipe years ago, and then found it and sent it to me right away. You can easily substitute walnuts or pecans, but no matter what you choose, you're sure to love it.

1 c. sugar
1/4 c. evaporated milk
1 T. water
1/8 t. salt

1/2 t. cinnamon
1/2 t. vanilla extract
2-1/4 c. cashews

Combine sugar, evaporated milk, water, salt, cinnamon and vanilla. Bring to a boil over medium heat; boil until mixture reaches the soft-ball stage, or 234 to 243 degrees on a candy thermometer. Stir in cashews; turn out onto wax paper. Separate quickly using a fork. If nuts are stuck together after they are cooled, break them apart by hand. Store in an airtight container. Makes about 3 cups.

Guests will feel cozy on a wintry night if you make their beds with flannel sheets...so soft and snuggly.

WELCOME
Friends

Chocolate Chip Cheese Ball

Janice Gavarkavich
Martins Ferry, OH

*For color and variety, use mini candy coated chocolates
instead of chocolate chips.*

8-oz. pkg. cream cheese,
  softened
1/2 c. butter, softened
1/4 t. vanilla extract
3/4 c. powdered sugar
2 T. brown sugar, packed

3/4 c. mini semi-sweet
  chocolate chips
3/4 c. pecans or walnuts,
  finely chopped
graham cracker sticks

Blend cream cheese, butter and vanilla in a mixing bowl until fluffy.
Gradually add sugars; beat just until combined. Stir in chocolate chips.
Cover and refrigerate for 2 hours. Place on a large piece of plastic wrap;
shape into a ball. Refrigerate for at least one additional hour. At serving
time, roll ball in chopped nuts. Serve with graham cracker sticks for
dipping. Makes about 2 cups.

Invite your neighbors over for an old-fashioned tree-trimming party.
Play your favorite holiday music, serve lots of yummy snacks, and
before you know it everyone will be in the holiday spirit!

Scrumptious Chocolate Eggnog

Marlene Darnell
Newport Beach, CA

An absolute must for all chocolate lovers!

4 pasteurized eggs, separated
1/2 c. brown sugar, packed
2/3 c. baking cocoa
1 T. vanilla extract
1-1/2 c. milk
1/2 c. rum or milk

1/8 t. salt
1-1/2 c. whipping cream,
　whipped
Garnish: 1/3 c. semi-sweet
　baking chocolate, grated

Beat together egg yolks, brown sugar, cocoa and vanilla until thick and smooth. Slowly stir in milk and rum or milk. Mix well. Cover; refrigerate until ready to serve, at least 2 hours. In a large bowl, beat egg whites with salt until soft peaks form. Fold whipped cream into chocolate mixture; gently fold in egg whites. Garnish with grated chocolate; serve immediately. Serves 6 to 8.

Fill vintage-style milk bottles with homemade eggnog or cocoa,
set them in a wire milk bottle carrier and deliver
to friends...what a tasty gift!

WELCOME
Friends

Mocha Cocoa

Molly Cool
Gooseberry Patch

*A blend of bittersweet chocolate and coffee
make this unbelieveable.*

2 c. milk
4 1-oz. sqs. bittersweet baking
   chocolate, chopped
2 T. sugar
1/8 t. salt

2 T. baking cocoa
1-1/2 c. hot brewed coffee
1 c. light cream
1 T. almond extract
Garnish: whipped topping

Combine milk and chocolate in a heavy saucepan over medium heat.
Heat mixture until chocolate is completely dissolved and smooth,
whisking constantly. Stir in sugar, salt and cocoa. Bring mixture to a
simmer; add hot coffee and cream. Simmer for 5 minutes. Remove
from heat; add almond extract. Top with dollops of whipped topping.
Serve immediately. Serves 4 to 6.

Sponge water-soluble acrylic paint over paper doilies and you'll
get the sweetest snowflake designs on windows. After winter,
they easily wipe off with a damp sponge.

Ham & Spinach Roll-Ups

Dorothy Lester
Hickory Hills, IL

These roll-ups have a dash of Dijon mustard,
which really adds flavor.

10-3/4 oz. can cream of celery
   soup
8-oz. container sour cream
1 T. Dijon mustard
1 c. instant rice, uncooked
10-oz. pkg. frozen chopped
   spinach, thawed and drained
8-oz. container small-curd
   cottage cheese

2 eggs, beaten
1/2 c. onion, chopped
1/4 c. all-purpose flour
18 slices deli boiled ham
Garnish: bread crumbs and
   paprika

Mix soup, sour cream and mustard together; set aside. In another bowl, combine 1/2 cup of the soup mixture, rice, spinach, cottage cheese, eggs, onion and flour; mix well. Place 2 tablespoons of spinach mixture on each slice of ham; roll up. Arrange rolls seam-side down in an 11"x7" baking pan; spoon remaining soup mixture over ham. Top with crumbs and paprika; bake, uncovered, at 350 degrees for 30 to 35 minutes. Let stand 10 minutes before serving. Makes 18.

For a holiday surprise, hang a sprig of mistletoe in your doorway!

WELCOME
Friends

Blue Cheese-Bacon Puffs

Robin Hill
Rochester, NY

*These puffs freeze well too. Just thaw in refrigerator overnight
and reheat at 350 degrees for 5 minutes.*

1-1/2 c. water
1/2 c. butter
1-1/2 c. all-purpose flour
1/2 t. salt
1/4 t. pepper
1/4 t. cayenne pepper

6 eggs
2 4-oz. pkgs. blue cheese
8 slices bacon, crisply cooked
    and crumbled
4 green onions, finely chopped

Heat water and butter in a large saucepan over medium-high heat;
bring to a boil. Add flour and seasonings; cook, stirring with a wooden
spoon, until mixture leaves sides of pan and forms a smooth ball of
dough. Remove from heat; cool 4 to 5 minutes. Add eggs, one at a
time, beating well after each addition. Blend in cheese, bacon and
onions. Drop by rounded teaspoonfuls about 2 inches apart on lightly
greased baking sheets. Bake at 400 degrees for 20 to 25 minutes, or
until golden. Serve warm or at room temperature. Makes 6 dozen.

Set fragrant gingerbread men across your mantel
or windowsill for a bit of old-fashioned fun.

Holiday Ham Dip

Tracy Brookshire
Champaign, IL

A blend of 3 cheeses and ham...what flavor!

2 8-oz. pkgs. cream cheese,
    softened
5-oz. jar sharp pasteurized
    process cheese spread
1 c. shredded Cheddar cheese
8-oz. container sour cream

1/8 t. Worcestershire sauce
2 8-oz. pkgs. deli ham, diced
3 bunches green onions,
    chopped
1 loaf Hawaiian bread, cubed

Mix cheeses, sour cream and Worcestershire sauce in a microwave-safe bowl; heat until creamy. Mix well; stir in ham and onions. Serve with bread cubes for dipping. Makes about 7 cups.

Spoon dips and spreads into pretty crocks or vintage blue canning
jars, they're ideal as hostess gifts. Don't forget to tie on
a spreader too...she'll love it!

WELCOME
Friends

Pizzeria Pizza Dip

Jessica Parker
Mulvane, KS

With all the taste of your favorite pizza!

2 8-oz. pkgs. cream cheese
14-oz. jar pizza sauce
1 c. shredded mozzarella cheese

1/4 c. pepperoni, diced
1 loaf French bread, sliced

Place unwrapped blocks of cream cheese side by side in a glass pie plate or baking pan. Pour pizza sauce over cream cheese; sprinkle with mozzarella cheese and pepperoni. Bake at 350 degrees for 20 to 25 minutes or microwave on high setting for 6 to 8 minutes, until hot and bubbly. Serve with slices of bread for dipping. Makes 8 to 10 servings.

Remember the birds at Christmastime. Decorate an outdoor tree with suet balls, birdseed bells, garlands of fruit and hollowed-out orange halves filled with birdseed.

Garlicky Hot Wings

Linda Nichols
Wintersville, OH

Everyone loves wings, and this recipe makes it easy
for you to serve them any time!

2-oz. bottle hot pepper sauce
2 cloves garlic, minced
1-1/2 t. dried rosemary
1 t. dried thyme
1/4 t. salt

1/4 t. pepper
2-1/2 lbs. chicken wings
Optional: celery stalks, carrot
   sticks and blue cheese salad
   dressing

Combine hot pepper sauce, garlic and seasonings; mix well. Add chicken wings; toss to coat evenly. Arrange wings in a lightly greased 13"x9" baking pan: bake at 425 degrees for 30 to 40 minutes, or until juices run clear, turning every 10 minutes. Serve with celery stalks, carrot sticks and blue cheese dressing, if desired. Makes about 2 dozen.

If you're hosting a holiday dinner, tie up a stack of cookies
with ribbon and set at each place setting.
A sweet treat for guests!

Tex-Mex Mini Chicken Cups

Trisha Fipps
Dunbar, WI

*I usually mix up the ingredients for the filling ahead of time,
then put them together right before company arrives.*

1-1/2 lbs. boneless, skinless
  chicken breasts, cooked
  and shredded
1 c. ranch salad dressing or
  sour cream
1/4 t. salt
1/4 t. pepper
8-oz. pkg. shredded Monterey
  Jack cheese

2 T. chili powder
24 wonton wrappers
1 c. red or green pepper, finely
  chopped
Optional: salsa, sour cream,
  guacamole

Combine chicken, salad dressing or sour cream, salt and pepper; set aside. In a separate bowl, combine cheese with chili powder; set aside. Press each wonton wrapper into a lightly greased muffin cup. Bake at 350 degrees for 5 minutes, or until lightly golden; remove from oven and cool. Spoon one tablespoon chicken filling into each wonton cup; sprinkle with cheese mixture and top with chopped pepper. Return to oven; bake for an additional 10 minutes, or until cheese is melted. Serve with salsa, sour cream and guacamole, if desired. Makes 2 dozen.

Clever giftwrap...try funny pages, maps, fabric or copies of
the kids' artwork. Grandma will love it!

Apple-Cranberry Sparkler

Janice Miller
Huntington, IN

This has a sweet-tart flavor your guests will love.

2 c. water
4 teabags
1 c. cranberry juice cocktail

1 c. apple juice
2 t. sugar

In a saucepan, bring water to boil over medium-high heat; add teabags. Brew tea for 5 minutes; remove and discard teabags. Combine tea, juice and sugar in a pitcher. Stir until sugar dissolves; chill. Makes one quart.

New neighbors on the block? Surprise them with a cheery red enamelware pail filled with warm muffins, cocoa mix, marshmallows and fresh fruit...what a welcome!

WELCOME
Friends

Cheery Christmas Coffee

Kay Marone
Des Moines, IA

Spiced coffee with a surprising orange twist!

1/3 c. ground coffee
1/2 t. cinnamon
1/8 t. ground cloves

1/4 c. orange marmalade
3 c. water
Optional: sugar

Place coffee, cinnamon and cloves in filter in brew basket of coffee maker. Place marmalade in empty coffee pot. Brew coffee as usual with water. When brewing is complete, mix well. Pour into coffee mugs; serve with sugar, if desired. Serves 6.

Homemade coupons are great stocking stuffers for the entire family! How about coupons promising to make dinner so Mom can put her feet up, or shovel the driveway for Dad?

Jo Ann's Holiday Brie

Jo Ann

*One of my favorite holiday recipes...great for "pop-in" guests
because it's so quick & easy to prepare.*

13.2-oz. pkg. Brie cheese
1/4 c. caramel ice cream topping
1/2 c. sweetened, dried
   cranberries

1/2 c. dried apricots, chopped
1/2 c. chopped pecans
assorted crackers

Place Brie on an ungreased microwave-safe dish; microwave on high
setting for 10 to 15 seconds. Cut out a wedge to see if center is soft.
If center is still firm, return cheese to microwave for another 5 to
10 seconds, or until cheese is soft and spreadable. Watch carefully,
as the center will begin to melt quickly. Drizzle with caramel topping;
sprinkle with cranberries, apricots and nuts. Serve with crackers.
Makes 6 to 8 servings.

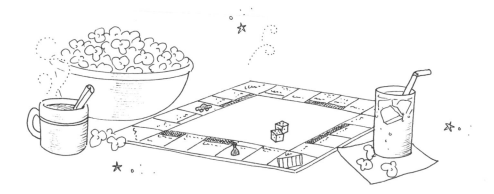

Stay in on a snowy night...fill the table with lots of tasty snacks and
pull out a board game or two. What fun for the entire family!

WELCOME
Friends

Creamy Crab Spread

*We can't get enough of this spread...I get requests
all the time for this recipe!*

1/3 c. mayonnaise
1/3 c. chili sauce
1 T. prepared horseradish
1 clove garlic, minced
1/2 t. mustard
1/4 to 1/2 t. hot pepper sauce

1/2 t. salt
2 6-oz. cans crabmeat, drained
2 eggs, hard-boiled, peeled
   and finely chopped
assorted crackers

Combine first 7 ingredients; mix well. Stir in crabmeat and eggs.
Cover and refrigerate for at least 2 hours. Serve with crackers.
Makes 2-1/2 cups.

Set a jar of Creamy Crab Spread and assorted crackers inside
a child's sand pail for gift-giving...how clever!

It's Snow Fun...
get-togethers with family & friends.

Christmas Ornament Exchange...
friends bring an ornament to swap.

Dessert Party...everyone
brings their best ooey-gooey
dessert to share.

Decorating Party...get together
to deck the halls, walls
and mantels!

Caroling...don't worry if you're
off key; you'll sound terrific!

Progressive dinner...begin by
enjoying appetizers at one home,
then move on to visit other homes
for the salad, soup, main course
and dessert.

Card or Tag-making...ask friends
to bring buttons, ribbon, stamps,
rick rack, pretty papers and
decorative-edged scissors to make
sweet Christmas cards and tags.

Gingerbread House Building...always
a fun family get-together!

Cozy Kitchen
SUPPERS

Cheesy Chicken Chowder

Sue Busse
Marysville, OH

*Warm up after snowman building with a big bowl of
this creamy soup.*

2 c. chicken broth
2 c. potatoes, peeled and diced
1/2 c. carrots, peeled and sliced
1/2 c. celery, sliced
1/2 c. onion, chopped
1/2 t. salt

1/4 t. pepper
1/4 c. butter
1/4 c. all-purpose flour
2 c. milk
2 c. shredded Cheddar cheese
1 c. cooked chicken, diced

Bring chicken broth to a boil in a stockpot over medium-high heat.
Add vegetables, salt and pepper; cover and simmer for 10 minutes. Set
aside. Melt butter in a second stockpot over low heat; add flour and
mix well. Gradually add milk, stirring constantly until thickened. Add
shredded cheese, chicken and broth mixture; heat through without
boiling. Makes 6 to 8 servings.

When you share a pot of homemade soup with neighbors,
include a stack of bowls tied with a festive ribbon.
A warming welcome on the first snowfall.

Christmas Eve Soup

Jessica Heimbaugh
Gilbert, IA

I am 11 years old and my mom and I had so much fun making recipes from one of your cookbooks, I wanted to share one of our favorites with you. We always have this soup on Christmas Eve, and hope you will enjoy it as much as our family does.

2 c. potatoes, peeled and diced
1/2 c. carrot, peeled and diced
1/2 c. celcry, chopped
1/4 c. onion, chopped
2 c. water
1-1/2 t. salt
1/4 t. pepper

1 c. cooked ham, cubed
1/4 c. margarine
1/4 c. all-purpose flour
2 c. milk
8-oz. pkg. shredded Cheddar
   cheese

Combine first 7 ingredients in a large soup pot; bring to a boil over medium heat. Reduce heat; cover and simmer until vegetables are tender. Stir in ham; set aside. In a separate saucepan, melt margarine; stir in flour until smooth. Gradually add milk; bring to a boil. Cook and stir for 2 minutes, until thickened. Stir in cheese until melted; add to vegetable mixture and heat through. Serves 8.

Fill a jar with hearty soup, then wrap it up with a woolly
scarf...perfect for your letter carrier on a frosty day.
Don't forget the spoon!

Very Veggie Bean Soup

Carole Anne Barbaro
Clayton, NJ

Loaded with good-for-you vegetables!

7-oz. turkey Kielbasa, halved
   lengthwise and cut into
   1/2-inch pieces
1 c. baby carrots, halved
1 c. onion, chopped
2 cloves garlic, minced
4 c. chicken broth

2 15-1/2 oz. cans Great
   Northern beans, drained
   and rinsed
1/2 t. Italian seasoning
1/2 t. pepper
6-oz. pkg. baby spinach leaves

Spray a large saucepan with non-stick vegetable spray. Add Kielbasa, carrots, onion and garlic; sauté over medium heat for 3 minutes, stirring occasionally. Reduce heat to medium; simmer for 5 minutes. Add broth, beans, Italian seasoning and pepper. Bring to a boil; reduce heat and simmer for 5 to 10 minutes. Place 2 cups soup in a food processor or blender; process until smooth. Return puréed soup to saucepan; simmer for 5 minutes. Remove from heat. Add spinach, stirring until spinach wilts. Makes 4 to 6 servings.

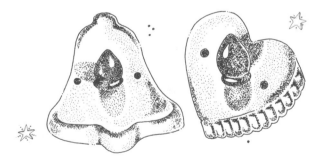

Make croutons in no time. Brush bread with butter, cut with mini cookie cutters and sprinkle on your favorite dried herbs. Simply bake at 300 degrees until crispy.

Chili with Corn Dumplings

Tanya Graham
Lawrenceville, GA

So simple yet so satisfying.

1-1/2 lbs. ground beef	2 T. chili powder
3/4 c. onion, chopped	1 t. garlic, minced
15-oz. can corn, divided	1-1/3 c. biscuit baking mix
16-oz. can stewed tomatoes	2/3 c. cornmeal
16-oz. can tomato sauce	2/3 c. milk
1 t. hot pepper sauce	3 T. fresh cilantro, chopped

Brown ground beef and onion in a Dutch oven over medium heat;
drain. Set aside 1/2 cup corn; stir remaining corn with liquid, tomatoes,
sauces, chili powder and garlic into beef mixture. Heat
to boiling. Reduce heat; cover and simmer for 15 minutes. Mix
baking mix and cornmeal in a medium bowl; stir in milk, cilantro
and reserved corn just until moistened. Drop dough by rounded
tablespoonfuls onto simmering chili. Cook over low heat, uncovered,
for 15 minutes. Cover and cook an additional 15 to 18 minutes,
until dumplings are dry on top. Makes 6 servings.

For a quick country gift in no
time, fill a canning jar with
vintage-style mini ornaments,
or cranberries and sprigs of
fragrant greenery. A glass
votive holder will sit nicely
inside the jar rim. Finish the
gift off by tucking in a tealight.

Cranberry Upside-Down Muffins

Barbara Girlardo
Pittsburgh, PA

Served warm, these tangy muffins are delicious alongside savory soups and stews.

2-1/2 c. all-purpose flour
1/2 c. sugar
1 T. baking powder
1/2 t. salt

1-1/4 c. milk
1/3 c. butter, melted
1 egg, beaten

Combine flour, sugar, baking powder and salt in a large bowl; mix well. Add milk, butter and egg; stir just until moistened. Set aside. Prepare Cranberry Topping; spoon into 18 greased muffin cups. Spoon batter over topping, filling each cup 2/3 full. Bake at 400 degrees for 20 to 25 minutes, until a toothpick tests clean. Immediately invert onto a wire rack set over wax paper; serve warm. Makes 1-1/2 dozen.

Cranberry Topping:

1/3 c. brown sugar, packed
1/4 c. butter
1/2 t. cinnamon

1/2 c. cranberries, halved
1/2 c. chopped nuts

Combine ingredients in a small saucepan. Cook over medium heat until brown sugar is dissolved.

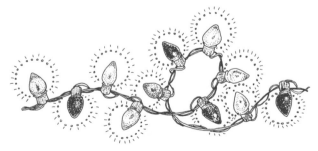

I am in holiday humor!

- William Shakespeare

Nutty Brown Sugar Muffins

Pearl Weaver
East Prairie, MO

So much like pecan pie, sure to become a new favorite.

2 eggs, beaten
1/2 c. butter, melted
1 c. brown sugar, packed

1/2 c. all-purpose flour
1 c. chopped pecans

Stir together eggs and butter. Add remaining ingredients; stir just until blended. Spray foil muffin cup liners with non-stick vegetable spray; fill muffin cups 2/3 full. Bake at 350 degrees for 25 minutes. Remove muffins from pan immediately; cool. Makes 10.

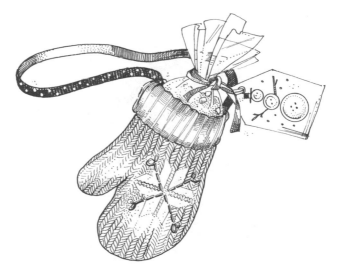

Give Nutty Brown Sugar Muffins tucked inside a stocking or mitten.
Wrap each muffin in plastic wrap, then slip inside...yum!

Savory Winter Stew

Marla Arbet
Burlington, WI

*A steaming cup of this stew is perfect to enjoy
before a day of holiday shopping!*

1 lb. Polish sausage, sliced	4 c. water
1 onion, sliced	2 c. red cabbage, shredded
8-oz. pkg. sliced mushrooms	2 T. rice vinegar
1 yellow squash, cubed	1 T. brown sugar, packed
1 clove garlic, minced	2 t. chicken bouillon granules
1 T. oil	1/8 t. pepper

Over medium heat in a large saucepan, cook sausage, onion, mushrooms, squash and garlic in oil for 5 minutes, until vegetables are tender; add remaining ingredients. Bring to a boil; reduce heat to a simmer for 15 to 20 minutes. Serves 5.

Stitch up some plump homespun hearts and set in a bowl by the door. Your friends & family will love choosing one to take home as a reminder of their visit.

Red Barn Chowder

Suzanne Pottker
Elgin, IL

*A delicious, hearty chowder...there's nothing better
on a frosty afternoon.*

1 lb. hot Italian sausage,
   broken up
1 onion, chopped
3 stalks celery, chopped
1 green pepper, choppcd
1 red pepper, chopped
2 zucchini, quartered and sliced
3 to 4 cloves garlic, chopped

28-oz. can stewed tomatoes
10-oz. can tomatoes with
   green chiles
18-oz. can tomato paste
2 t. dried basil
salt and pepper to taste
1 c. canned garbanzo beans,
   drained and rinsed

Combine sausage, onion, celery, peppers, zucchini and garlic in a large
saucepan; sauté until sausage is browned and vegetables are tender.
Stir in tomatoes, tomato paste, basil, salt and pepper; heat until cooked
through. Mix in garbanzo beans; heat through. Serves 6.

When taking gifts to neighbors, set them in a cheery red
wagon...the kids will have a ball pulling it from door-to-door
and singing carols along the way!

Mee-Mee's Berry Gelatin

Brooke Steinke
Williams, CA

*Mee-Mee, my great-grandmother, first made this gelatin recipe
and now it's just not Thanksgiving and Christmas without it!*

3.4-oz. pkg. raspberry gelatin
  mix
3.4-oz. pkg. lemon gelatin mix
2 c. boiling water
10-oz. pkg. frozen raspberries,
  thawed

1 c. whole-berry cranberry sauce
8-oz. can crushed pineapple,
  drained
1 c. lemon-lime soda

In a mixing bowl, dissolve gelatin mixes in boiling water; stir well. Add
raspberries and cranberry sauce; mix well. Stir in pineapple. Let cool
briefly. Add soda; pour into a 9"x9" serving dish and refrigerate until
set. Spread Vanilla Topping over top of gelatin. Serves 6.

Vanilla Topping:

3-1/2 oz. pkg. instant vanilla
  pudding mix
1 c. milk

2 c. frozen whipped topping,
  thawed

Place half of pudding mix in a medium bowl, reserving the rest for
another recipe. Beat milk into pudding mix; fold in topping.

At last the dinner was all done, the cloth was cleaned, the hearth
swept and the fire made up. A Merry Christmas to us all,
my dears. God bless us! Which all the family re-echoed.
God bless us every one.

- Charles Dickens

Winter Fruit Salad

Leah Caplan
Fairfax, VA

This refreshing and pretty salad is an all-around family favorite.

2 oranges, peeled and sectioned
1 grapefruit, peeled and
   sectioned
2 apples, cored, peeled and diced
2 pears, cored, peeled and diced
2 bananas, sliced

1 c. purple seedless grapes
1 c. apple cider
1 T. lemon juice
1-1/2 c. mayonnaise
6 leaves lettuce

Mix together all fruits; stir in cider and lemon juice. Chill for 2 to 3 hours. Drain, reserving juice. Combine mayonnaise and 1/3 cup reserved fruit juice. Arrange fruit on lettuce leaves; drizzle with mayonnaise mixture. Serves 6.

Kids love camping out under the Christmas tree! Lay sleeping bags, quilts and pillows around the tree and watch a favorite holiday movie together.

Cream of Wild Rice Soup

Geralyn Hurley
McFarland, WI

So tasty served with homemade bread or rolls.

1/4 c. butter
1 onion, chopped
1 carrot, peeled and shredded
1 stalk celery, chopped
1/2 c. all-purpose flour
6 to 8 c. chicken broth
6.2-oz. pkg. long-grain and wild
   rice mix, cooked

1 c. cooked chicken breast,
   cubed
1/4 t. salt
1/4 t. pepper
1 c. evaporated milk
1/4 c. fresh chives, snipped

Melt butter in a large saucepan over medium heat. Add onion, carrot and celery; cook until tender. Stir in flour until blended; gradually add broth. Stir in cooked rice, chicken, salt and pepper. Bring to a boil over medium heat; cook and stir for 2 minutes, or until thickened. Stir in milk; cook for an additional 3 to 5 minutes. Sprinkle with chives. Serves 10.

Toss a bundle of cinnamon sticks or orange peel into
a crackling fire for a delightful fragrance.

Holiday Best Oyster Stew

Teresa Stiegelmeyer
Indianapolis, IN

*We serve this for Thanksgiving, Christmas Eve
and any other cold wintry evening!*

1/2 c. butter
1 c. celery, chopped
1 c. onion, chopped
7-oz. can sliced mushrooms,
　　drained
1 pt. oysters
10-3/4 oz. can cream of potato
　　soup

4 c. milk
1 pt. half-and-half
1 t. salt
1 t. pepper
Garnish: paprika or dried parsley

Heat butter in a large soup pot over medium heat. Add celery and
onion; cook until tender. Stir in mushrooms and oysters with their
liquid; cook until edges of oysters curl, about 5 minutes. Add soup,
milk, half-and-half, salt and pepper. Heat through without boiling.
Garnish with paprika or parsley. Serves 6 to 8.

Bundle up the kids and take a ride to see the holiday lights
around town. Bring cozy blankets, plump pillows...the kids
can even wear their jammies!

Divine Seafood Chowder

Audrey Laudenat
East Haddam, CT

This chowder is a meal all by itself!

1 onion, sliced
4 potatoes, peeled and sliced
minced garlic to taste
1 t. dill weed
2 T. butter
1 c. clam juice, heated to boiling

15-oz. can creamed corn
salt and pepper to taste
1/2 lb. haddock or cod fillet
1/2 lb. medium raw shrimp,
    peeled, cleaned and halved
1 c. light cream, warmed

Layer all ingredients except cream in a slow cooker, placing fish and shrimp on top. Cover and cook on high setting for one hour; reduce setting to low and cook for 3 hours. Add cream; stir gently and serve. Makes 4 to 6 servings.

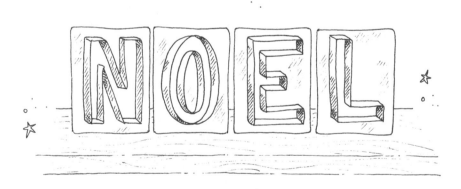

Cookie cutters in alphabet shapes are a clever way to spell out holiday greetings! Just line them up along a window, mantel or cupboard shelf.

Christmas Vegetable Soup

Diana Krol
Nickerson, KS

For many years we served this soup for our church's Christmas auction dinner, along with French bread and an assortment of pies for dessert. Not only is the soup deliciously hearty, it makes the entire church (or house!) smell wonderful.

3 T. oil
1 meaty beef soup bone
1 onion, chopped
1/8 to 1/4 t. turmeric
1-1/2 t. salt
1/8 t. pepper
1/8 t. dried thyme
1/8 t. dried sage
1/8 t. allspice

1 bay leaf
6 c. water
4 c. tomato juice
1 head cabbage, shredded
1 c. carrots, peeled and chopped
1 c. celery, chopped
1 c. potatoes, peeled and cubed
16-oz. can green beans

Heat oil in a large saucepan; brown soup bone and sauté onion. Remove soup bone to a slow cooker and set aside. Add just enough turmeric to saucepan to turn onion yellow. Stir in remaining seasonings; sauté over low heat for a few minutes. Add to slow cooker along with remaining ingredients. Cover and cook on low setting for 8 hours. Remove soup bone; chop off meat and return to soup. Discard bay leaf; skim any fat. Makes 10 servings.

A cheery Santa hat is the ideal spot to hold all
the holiday cards you receive!

Hot Bacon-Potato Salad

Amber Erskine
Hartland, VT

This salad is just right for toting to a family get-together or social.

1/4 lb. bacon, crisply cooked,
   crumbled and drippings
   reserved
3/4 c. celery, sliced
1/2 c. onion, chopped
1-1/2 T. all-purpose flour
3/4 c. water

1/3 c. vinegar
2 T. sugar
1-1/2 t. salt
1 t. mustard
1/4 t. celery seed
4 c. potatoes, peeled, cooked
   and sliced

Heat reserved drippings over medium heat in a large skillet. Add celery and onion; cook until tender. Add remaining ingredients except potatoes and bacon; cook until thickened, stirring constantly. Fold in potatoes and bacon; heat through. Serve warm. Makes 4 to 6 servings.

Enjoy every magical moment...help little ones write a letter
to Santa, leave out milk & cookies, along with carrots for
the reindeer. These are the days you'll always remember.

Irene's Layered Salad

Irene Robinson
Cincinnati, OH

*Your family will love this make-ahead salad so much,
there won't be any leftovers!*

1/2 c. mayonnaise
1 T. sugar
1/4 t. salt
1/4 t. pepper
6 c. mixed salad greens
1 red onion, sliced

10-oz. pkg. frozen peas, thawed
8-oz. pkg. sliced Swiss cheese,
   cut into thin strips
1 lb. bacon, crisply cooked
   and crumbled

Combine mayonnaise, sugar, salt and pepper in a small bowl; set aside.
In a large salad bowl, layer one-third of the greens and one-third each
of mayonnaise mixture, onion, peas and cheese. Repeat layering twice.
Cover and refrigerate for at least 2 hours. At serving time, add bacon
and toss. Makes 6 to 8 servings.

Open Christmas cards at suppertime so everyone can read
and enjoy them together!

Chicken & Noodles Stew

Janelle Sisley
Edinboro, PA

I have always loved stews; however, my fiancée didn't. It soon became my mission to create a stew he would love and I succeeded when I came up with this recipe! To make it even more flavorful, cook the chicken in low-sodium chicken broth instead of water.

3 to 3-1/2 lbs. chicken
28-oz. can whole tomatoes, chopped
3 cloves garlic, chopped
2 bay leaves
salt and pepper to taste
1 onion, coarsely chopped
3 to 4 carrots, peeled and coarsely chopped
4 stalks celery, coarsely chopped
1 head cabbage, coarsely chopped
10-oz. pkg. frozen green beans
10-oz. pkg. frozen corn
3 c. cooked medium egg noodles
2 T. sugar

Combine chicken, tomatoes and juice, garlic, bay leaves, salt and pepper in a large stockpot. Add enough water to just cover the chicken; simmer over low to medium heat until chicken juices run clear when pierced. Remove chicken, reserving broth in stockpot, and let cool; remove and discard bones. Cut into bite-size pieces; refrigerate. Add onion, carrots, celery and cabbage to broth in stockpot; add more water if needed to cover vegetables. Bring to a boil; reduce to a simmer and cook for 2-1/2 hours. Add chicken, green beans, corn, cooked noodles, sugar, and additional salt and pepper to taste. Simmer for an additional 15 minutes. Discard bay leaves before serving. Makes 4 to 6 servings.

Whip up a cozy fleece blanket for snuggling under in no time at all. Cut fleece to any size and use scissors to add a fringe to the edge...so easy, no sewing needed!

Broccoli-Cheddar Soup

Lisa Peterson
Sabina, OH

I know I can count on this yummy soup
when I want something extra-special.

1-1/2 c. water
10-oz. pkg. frozen broccoli,
   thawed
2 T. butter
1 cube chicken bouillon
2 T. dried, minced onion
2-1/4 c. milk, divided
10-3/4 oz. can Cheddar cheese
   soup

1 c. shredded Cheddar cheese
1/2 t. Worcestershire sauce
1/8 t. salt
1/8 t. pepper
1/8 t. garlic salt
2 T. all-purpose flour

Combine water, broccoli, butter, bouillon cube and onion in a stockpot; cook over medium heat until onion is tender. Add 2 cups milk, soup, cheese, Worcestershire sauce, salt, pepper and garlic salt; cook over low heat until cheese melts. Stir in flour and remaining milk; heat until thickened. Serves 4.

Arrange sparkly ornaments on a cake stand, dust with glittery
mica snow, then cover with a bell jar...so charming.

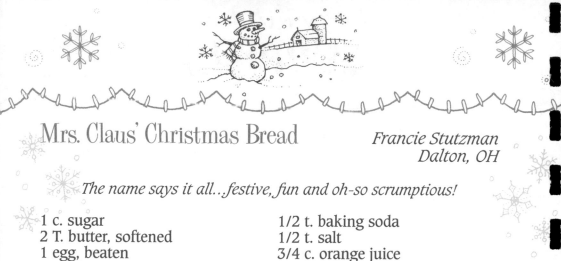

Mrs. Claus' Christmas Bread

Francie Stutzman
Dalton, OH

The name says it all...festive, fun and oh-so scrumptious!

1 c. sugar
2 T. butter, softened
1 egg, beaten
2 c. all-purpose flour
1 t. baking powder

1/2 t. baking soda
1/2 t. salt
3/4 c. orange juice
1 c. cranberries, chopped
1/2 c. chopped nuts

Blend together sugar, butter and egg. Add remaining ingredients; mix well and pour into a greased 9"x5" loaf pan. Bake at 350 degrees for 45 to 50 minutes. Makes one loaf.

Spring-type clothespins are just right for keeping strands of lights in place! Spray paint them green and let dry...so easy.

Orange Marmalade Bread

Linda Behling
Cecil, PA

I like to keep several loaves on hand to serve when friends drop by.

1/2 c. margarine, softened	2 t. baking powder
1/2 c. brown sugar, packed	1/2 t. baking soda
2 eggs	1 t. salt
10-oz. jar orange marmalade	1/2 c. orange juice
2-3/4 c. all-purpose flour	1/2 c. chopped nuts

Beat together margarine and sugar until light and fluffy. Add eggs, one at a time, mixing well. Blend in marmalade; set aside. Combine flour, baking powder, baking soda and salt. Add dry ingredients to margarine mixture alternately with orange juice; stir in nuts. Pour into a greased and floured 9"x5" loaf pan. Bake at 350 degrees for about one hour, or until toothpick tests clean. Cool 15 minutes before removing from pan. Makes one loaf.

If you're planning to string popcorn as a tree garland, pop it a couple days before you plan to string it and it will hold up nicely.

Turkey Soup Williamsburg Style

Jan Sofranko
Malta, IL

*A recipe shared with me by a friend who lived next door to me
20 years ago...and I've served it at my table ever since then.*

3 onions, chopped
3 stalks celery, chopped
2 carrots, peeled and chopped
2 c. water
1 c. butter
1 c. all-purpose flour

2-1/2 qts. turkey broth
1 pt. half-and-half
1 c. cooked turkey, diced
1 c. cooked rice
salt and pepper to taste

Combine onions, celery, carrots and water in a saucepan; cook over
medium heat for 20 minutes. Set aside. In a large saucepan, melt
butter over low heat; blend in flour. Pour in broth and half-and-half;
cook until bubbly, about 4 to 5 minutes. Stir in vegetables. Cook for
10 minutes; add turkey and rice; sprinkle with salt and pepper. Cook
until heated through. Serves 10 to 12.

Have the kids build a snowman at Grandma's house while she's out
shopping...she'll be delighted!

Homestyle Vegetable Soup & Dumplings
Lois Bivens
Gooseberry Patch

Serve this old-fashioned favorite soup with warm rolls and real butter.

1/2 c. onion, chopped
1 T. oil
1/2 c. rosamarina or orzo pasta,
    uncooked
4 c. chicken or vegetable broth
16-oz. pkg. frozen peas,
    potatoes and carrots, thawed
15-1/2 oz. can Great Northern
    beans, drained and rinsed

1 t. dry mustard
1 c. biscuit baking mix
2/3 c. cornmeal
1/4 t. dried oregano
1/4 t. dried basil
2/3 c. milk

Sauté onion in oil over medium heat in a large saucepan until tender. Stir in pasta, broth, vegetables, beans and mustard; heat to boiling, stirring occasionally. In a mixing bowl, stir together baking mix, cornmeal and herbs; stir in milk just until moistened. Drop dough by tablespoonfuls onto boiling stew; reduce heat to low. Cook, uncovered, for 10 minutes. Cover and cook an additional 10 minutes. Serves 4.

Plastic cookie cutters, dipped in fabric paint, are so easy for
little ones to stamp onto napkins and tablecloths.

Chill Chaser Soup

Melissa Weber
Toledo, OH

*On blustery days, I always serve this soup with
a loaf of freshly baked bread.*

1 head cauliflower, chopped
4 potatoes, peeled and cubed
1/4 c. onion, chopped
2 qts. water
salt to taste

1/4 t. pepper
2 to 3 c. milk
8-oz. pkg. cream cheese,
   softened
1/4 c. butter

Combine cauliflower, potatoes, onion and water in a stockpot; cook
over medium-low heat for one hour. Mash slightly when soft; add
remaining ingredients. Simmer over low heat for 30 to 40 minutes.
Serves 6.

Fill a roomy stockpot with all the fixin's for a warming soup

supper...a ladle, soup mixes, favorite recipes and a big jar of

your best warm-you-to-your-toes chowder!

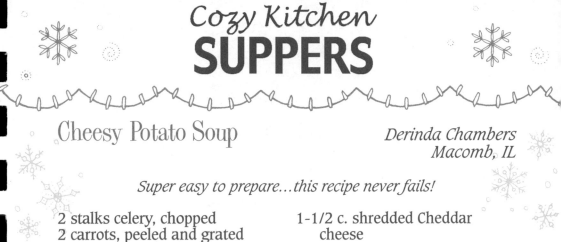

Cheesy Potato Soup

Derinda Chambers
Macomb, IL

Super easy to prepare...this recipe never fails!

2 stalks celery, chopped
2 carrots, peeled and grated
1/2 c. onion, chopped
1 T. butter
2 10-1/2 oz. cans chicken broth
2 10-3/4 oz. cans cream of
   potato soup

1-1/2 c. shredded Cheddar
   cheese
3/4 c. sour cream
salt and pepper to taste

In a large saucepan, sauté celery, carrots and onion in butter. Add broth; simmer for 20 minutes. Stir in soup, cheese and sour cream. Simmer 15 minutes longer; add salt and pepper to taste. Serves 6.

Don't forget to check the batteries in your camera...you don't want
to miss a single, magical Christmas moment!

Midwestern-Style Cornbread

Darlene Hartzler
Marshallville, OH

Top warm slices of cornbread with butter and you have an all-time favorite go-with for soups, stews and chowders!

1 c. sugar	1 c. buttermilk
3/4 c. shortening	1 t. baking soda
1 egg, beaten	1 c. all-purpose flour
1/8 t. salt	1 c. cornmeal

Mix all ingredients together; spoon into a lightly greased 13"x9" baking pan. Bake at 350 degrees for 25 to 30 minutes. Makes 9 servings.

Pair up a cast iron skillet and the ingredients for Midwestern-Style Cornbread for a cook on your gift list. Wrap it all up in a cheery red bandanna.

Cozy Kitchen
SUPPERS

Mom's Red Stew

Karen Boehme
Greensburg, PA

My mom always served this stew when we'd been playing in the snow for hours. It was a very welcome comfort food!

1 lb. stew beef, cubed
3 T. oil
26-oz. can tomato soup
4 to 5 c. water
1 stalk celery, sliced 1/2-inch
    thick

4 to 5 potatoes, peeled and
    cubed
3 to 4 carrots, peeled and sliced
    1/2-inch thick

Brown stew meat in oil in a large kettle. Add soup, water and celery; heat to boiling over medium heat. Reduce heat; add potatoes and carrots. Simmer slowly for 90 minutes to 2 hours, until vegetables are tender. Serves 4 to 6.

When college kids are coming home for Christmas, welcome them by decorating bedrooms with strands of twinkling lights!

Snow Days...
make it extra fun for the kids!

Set up a frosty scavenger hunt in the snow. Create a map and hide lots of waterproof surprises for the kids to find.

Make snow ice cream! Whip one cup heavy cream until soft peaks form, fold in 4 cups freshly fallen snow, then add sugar and vanilla extract to taste...yum!

Send the kids outside with gelatin molds, ice cream scoops, cake and bread pans so they can create the best-ever snow fort.

An absolute must-do... make snow angels!

Fabric crayons turn ordinary handkerchiefs into the sweetest gifts! Press a cotton or linen handkerchief with a hot iron, then let the kids create their own masterpieces. Lay a scrap piece of fabric over the drawing, and iron following the fabric crayon manufacturer's instructions. Decorated handkerchiefs are so pretty tied over jars of layered mixes, or tucked inside Christmas cards.

DINNER
at Grandma's

Herbed Roast Turkey Breast

Robin Lakin
LaPalma, CA

This is too good to serve only once or twice a year!

4 to 5-lb. turkey breast
1/4 c. fresh parsley, chopped
1 T. fresh thyme or rosemary,
    chopped
zest and juice of 1 lemon
2 tart apples, cored, peeled and
    chopped

2 stalks celery, cut in thirds
4 shallots, coarsely chopped
1 c. chicken broth
1/2 c. dry white wine or chicken
    broth
2 T. butter, softened
2 T. all-purpose flour

With your fingers, separate skin from turkey breast to make a pocket. Combine herbs and lemon zest; rub under skin. Pat skin back into place. Place apples, celery, shallots, broth and wine or broth in a slow cooker. Place turkey skin-side up on top; drizzle lemon juice over turkey. Cover and cook on low setting for 8 to 10 hours, or on high setting for 3-1/2 to 4 hours, until tender. Remove turkey; if desired, place in a preheated 450-degree oven for 5 to 10 minutes, until skin is golden. Transfer turkey to a serving platter and keep warm. Discard apples and celery; pour drippings into a skillet over medium heat. In a small bowl, combine butter and flour. Whisk into drippings; cook and stir until thickened and bubbly, about 15 minutes. Serve warm gravy with sliced turkey. Serves 4 to 6.

Keep an eye open at flea markets and tag sales for jelly molds and cake tins...dressed up with cellophane and ribbon, they're ideal for holding holiday treats to share.

DINNER
at Grandma's

Grandma's Holiday Stuffing

Wendy Lee Paffenroth
Pine Island, NY

Apples keep this stuffing moist.

1 large loaf day-old bread, torn
Optional: day-old corn muffins,
   broken up
1/2 c. butter
1 onion, diced
3 stalks celery, diced
Optional: 1/2 c. sliced
   mushrooms

2 tart apples, cored and diced
1/2 c. walnuts, coarsely chopped
1/2 c. raisins
1/2 to 3/4 c. water
1/2 to 1 T. poultry seasoning
dried parsley to taste
salt and pepper to taste

Place torn bread in a large baking dish; mix in muffins, if using.
Bake at 250 degrees for about 30 minutes, until dried out. Set aside.
Melt butter over low heat in a large skillet; sauté onion, celery and
mushrooms, if using, until tender. Add apples, walnuts and raisins;
stir to coat with butter. Mix in water and seasonings; pour over bread
and toss to moisten. Add a little more water if bread is very dry. Use
to stuff a 12 to 15-pound turkey before roasting; do not overstuff.
Or spread stuffing in a lightly greased 9"x5" baking pan and bake at
350 degrees for 30 to 40 minutes. Serves 8 to 10.

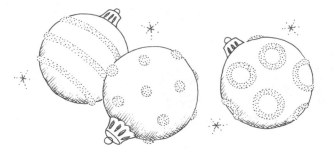

Randomly add dots of glue onto Christmas ball ornaments,
then sprinkle with glitter...frosty fun!

Chicken Oreganato

Annette Mullan
North Arlington, NJ

*Your kitchen will smell wonderful while this is baking!
For a nice meal, I like to serve roasted potatoes or
buttered noodles alongside servings.*

1/2 to 3/4 c. olive oil	salt and pepper to taste
1 c. red wine vinegar	dried oregano to taste
1/4 t. garlic powder	3 to 4 lbs. chicken
1/3 t. onion powder	1 onion, sliced

Combine olive oil, vinegar and seasonings in a bowl; add oregano to taste. Mix thoroughly. Transfer marinade to a large plastic zipping bag; add chicken and refrigerate 3 to 4 hours, or overnight. Spread onion in a lightly greased 13"x9" baking pan; arrange chicken on top, pouring remaining marinade over chicken. Sprinkle with additional oregano, if desired. Bake, covered, at 350 degrees for one to 1-1/2 hours. Uncover last 30 minutes to allow chicken to brown. Serves 4 to 6.

Tied with a bright red bow, a galvanized pail is just right
for filling with sand and dripless taper candles. Line up a few
along your porch steps for a festive welcome.

Pilafi

Jennie Gist
Gooseberry Patch

This Greek-style rice is such a nice addition to the dinner table.

2 c. long-cooking rice, uncooked
3-1/2 c. chicken broth
1 carrot, peeled and chopped
1 stalk celery, chopped
3/4 c. mushrooms, coarsely
  chopped

1 onion, chopped
1/8 t. paprika
1/8 t. salt
Optional: crumbled feta cheese

Bring rice and chicken broth to a boil over medium heat. Add vegetables; cook according to rice package directions, or until liquid is absorbed. Sprinkle with feta cheese, if desired. Serves 6.

Sprinkle glittery confetti in a large water-filled glass bowl,
then add floating candles...oh-so pretty!

Honeyed Raspberry Pork Chops

Elaine Slabinski
Monroe Township, NJ

*Raspberry jam pairs up with honey mustard
to make a flavorful sauce.*

4 boneless pork chops
2 T. all-purpose flour
1/3 c. honey mustard
1/4 c. raspberry jam

2 T. cider vinegar
1 T. olive oil
1 T. fresh parsley, chopped

Dredge pork chops in flour, shaking off any excess. In a small bowl, combine honey mustard, jam and vinegar; set aside. Heat oil in a large skillet over medium heat. Add pork chops and sauté until golden on both sides. Stir in mustard mixture; bring to a boil. Reduce heat and simmer for 10 minutes. Sprinkle with parsley. Serves 4.

Don't worry about having the perfect tablecloth. Crisply starched white sheets topped with candles of all shapes and sizes will cast a warm glow and make any table look magical.

DINNER
at Grandma's

Sunshine Carrots

Esther Elian
Skowhegan, ME

*A serving of these citrusy carrots will brighten up
the frostiest winter day!*

5 carrots, peeled
1 T. sugar
1 t. cornstarch
1/4 t. salt

1/4 t. ground ginger
1/4 c. orange juice
2 T. margarine

Cook carrots and set aside. Combine sugar, cornstarch, salt and ginger
in a small saucepan over medium heat. Add orange juice, stirring
constantly until thickened, about one minute. Stir in margarine.
Pour over carrots. Serves 4.

Topped with white butcher's paper and crayon placemats,
the kids' table will be so sweet! Leave crayons out for little
guests to add their own creative touches.

Aunt Millie's Meatloaf

Ida Vasily
Bethlehem, PA

This recipe has been in our family for over 50 years! It's been a consistently good old-fashioned recipe now serving a 4th generation. Every time I serve it, my family raves that it's the best meatloaf they've ever tasted. I know you'll agree once you've made it!

1 lb. ground beef or meatloaf
   mix
1 to 2 eggs, beaten
1 c. Italian-seasoned dry
   bread crumbs
1 onion, diced
1 T. dried parsley
1 T. catsup or tomato sauce

1 t. mustard
1 t. sugar
1/2 t. dried basil
1/8 t. salt
1/8 t. pepper
1/8 t. garlic powder
1 t. beef bouillon granules
1/2 c. boiling water

Combine all ingredients except bouillon and water in a large bowl; set aside. Dissolve bouillon in water; add to mixture and mix well. Form into a loaf; place in a greased 9"x5" loaf pan. Bake at 350 degrees for one hour. Makes 4 to 6 servings.

Miniature evergreens from a local nursery become the nicest placecard holders and ideal party favors.

Extra-Cheesy Macaroni & Cheese

Valarie Dennard
Palatka, FL

My husband says this is the best macaroni & cheese he's ever eaten!

8-oz. pkg. shredded Italian-
  blend cheese
8-oz. pkg. shredded sharp
  Cheddar cheese
2 eggs, beaten
12-oz. can evaporated milk
1-1/2 c. milk

1 t. salt
3/4 t. dry mustard
1/4 t. cayenne pepper
1/2 t. pepper
8-oz. pkg. small shell macaroni,
  uncooked

Combine cheeses in a large bowl; set aside. Whisk together eggs and next 6 ingredients in a large bowl; stir in macaroni and 3 cups cheese mixture. Pour macaroni mixture into a slow cooker; sprinkle with 3/4 cup cheese mixture. Cover and cook on low setting for 4 hours. Sprinkle servings with remaining cheese mixture. Serves 6 to 8.

Cheery chairs! Use a variety of ribbons to tie a large chenille candy cane to the back of each kitchen or dining room chair. Tuck in a sprig of greenery for a fresh holiday scent.

Grandmother's Ham & Beef Loaf

Diana Alton
Herrin, IL

A family favorite my grandmother, Otilia Lynch, always made for Sunday dinners and holidays.

2/3 lb. ground ham
1-1/2 lbs. ground beef
2 eggs, beaten
1 c. cracker crumbs

1 c. milk
1/4 t. pepper
2 T. brown sugar, packed
1/4 c. mustard

Combine ham, ground beef, eggs, cracker crumbs, milk and pepper in a large bowl; mix thoroughly. Spread mixture in a lightly greased 9"x5" loaf pan. Combine brown sugar and mustard; spread thin layer over loaf. Bake at 350 degrees for one hour. Serves 10.

The crisp color of green limes is so nice at Christmas. Fill a clear glass cannister or large jar with an assortment of whole limes, lime slices and sparkling water. A centerpiece in a snap!

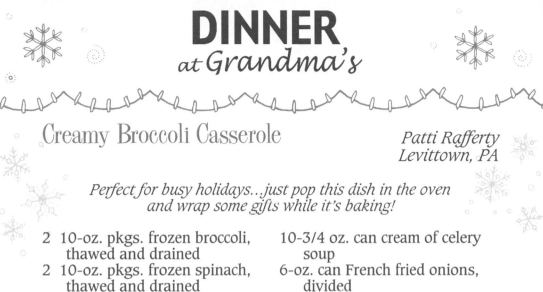

Creamy Broccoli Casserole

Patti Rafferty
Levittown, PA

*Perfect for busy holidays...just pop this dish in the oven
and wrap some gifts while it's baking!*

2 10-oz. pkgs. frozen broccoli,
  thawed and drained
2 10-oz. pkgs. frozen spinach,
  thawed and drained
10-3/4 oz. can cream of
  mushroom soup

10-3/4 oz. can cream of celery
  soup
6-oz. can French fried onions,
  divided
1/2 c. shredded Cheddar cheese

Combine first 4 ingredients in a large bowl; stir in half the French
fried onions. Pour into an ungreased 13"x9" baking pan; sprinkle
with remaining onions and cheese. Bake at 350 degrees for 30 to
45 minutes. Serves 8 to 10.

A quick-as-a-wink table runner...lay wide ribbon across
the table's length and width!

Chicken Ranch Fettuccine

Linda Teachey
Watha, NC

While the fettuccine is cooking, I toss the remaining ingredients together...quick and so delicious!

2 to 3 boneless, skinless chicken
   breasts, cooked and cubed
16-oz. pkg. fettuccine, cooked
10-oz. pkg. frozen broccoli,
   cooked

24-oz. bottle ranch salad
   dressing
Garnish: grated Parmesan
   cheese

Toss together all ingredients except Parmesan while fettuccine, chicken and broccoli are hot. Garnish with Parmesan cheese. Serves 6.

Give the kids visions of sugarplums! They will love this centerpiece for the kids' table. Wrap a sturdy box with paper, fill the box with gumdrops and insert lollipops into the candies.

Italian Zucchini Bake

Angie Venable
Gooseberry Patch

This colorful casserole bakes up with the tastiest
melted mozzarella topping.

2 T. butter
1 to 2 zucchini, chopped
1 onion, chopped
4 tomatoes, chopped

1 green pepper, chopped
Italian seasoning to taste
8-oz. pkg. shredded mozzarella
   cheese

Melt butter in a skillet over medium heat. Add zucchini and onion;
cook for 5 minutes, until onion is golden. Spoon zucchini mixture into
a lightly greased 2-quart casserole dish; stir in tomatoes, green pepper
and seasoning. Top with cheese. Bake at 350 degrees for 25 minutes,
or until cheese is melted. Serves 4.

Greet guests at your door with a clever welcome. Fill outdoor
urns with candles of all shapes and sizes. Add a colorful bow
and large jingle bells...that's it!

Brown Sugar-Glazed Ham

Dianna Pindell
Powell, OH

The glaze is what makes the difference!

1 c. brown sugar, packed
2 T. molasses
2 T. cornstarch

1 c. water
6-lb. fully-cooked honey ham

Combine brown sugar and molasses in a small saucepan; set aside. Mix together cornstarch and water; add to saucepan. Cook over medium heat until just bubbling, stirring occasionally. Remove from heat. Place ham in a roaster pan and carefully pour glaze over top. Cover ham with aluminum foil and bake at 350 degrees for 1-1/2 hours. Serves 10 to 12.

Tiered cake or pie plates, even a vintage iron egg holder are so nice for displaying tiny gifts, berries and greenery or votive candles.

Fruity Roasted Sweet Potatoes

Becca Brasfield
Burns, TN

With the addition of apples and cranberries, these sweet potatoes define comfort food.

3 sweet potatoes, peeled and
  cubed
2 Granny Smith apples, cored,
  peeled and cubed
2 T. olive oil
1 c. cranberries
1 T. honey

1-1/2 T. brown sugar, packed
1-1/2 T. chopped walnuts
1/4 c. sweetened flaked coconut
1 t. ground ginger
1 t. cinnamon
1/4 t. salt

Combine potatoes, apples and oil in a lightly greased 13"x9" baking pan. Mix well. Sprinkle cranberries on top of potato mixture and drizzle with honey. Bake at 450 degrees for 10 minutes. Reduce temperature to 350 degrees and bake for an additional 45 to 50 minutes, or until potatoes are tender. While casserole is baking, mix together brown sugar and next 5 ingredients. Remove casserole from oven and sprinkle brown sugar mixture over top. Return casserole to oven; bake for an additional 5 minutes. Serves 4 to 6.

Tartan fabric and a ribbon bow turn an ordinary paint can into a one-of-a-kind tin for homemade treats...just spray can with adhesive and cut fabric to fit. New paint cans are easily found at home-improvement stores...so clever!

Pepper-Crusted Roast Beef

Linda Behling
Cecil, PA

A caramelized brown sugar sauce is spooned over tender slices of beef.

2 to 3 lbs. boneless beef rib
   roast
1/4 c. garlic, minced
3 T. peppercorns
1/4 c. Worcestershire sauce

2 red onions, thinly sliced
1 T. oil
1 T. brown sugar, packed
2 T. balsamic vinegar

Rub roast with garlic and coat fat side of roast with peppercorns. Drizzle with Worcestershire sauce. Place in a roaster pan. Roast at 350 degrees for 40 minutes to one hour, or until meat thermometer reaches 150 degrees. Cook onions in oil in a small skillet over medium heat until onions are soft. Add brown sugar and vinegar; cook until caramelized, about 8 to 10 minutes. Slice roast; serve onions over top. Serves 6 to 8.

Place a guest book on the table alongside a jar filled with
colored pencils. Encourage everyone to sign it...kids can even
draw pictures. Add favorite photos and you'll have
a holiday scrapbook in no time!

DINNER
at Grandma's

Swiss-Onion Casserole

Bethany Simon
Lyford, TX

*You have to try this layered, crumb-topped
onion casserole...it's awesome!*

1/4 c. plus 2 T. butter, divided
3 sweet onions, chopped
8-oz. pkg. shredded Swiss
    cheese, divided
1 c. Italian-seasoned dry bread
    crumbs, divided

2 eggs
3/4 c. light cream
1 t. salt
1/8 t. pepper

Melt 1/4 cup butter in a large skillet over medium heat; add onions
and sauté until tender. Arrange half of onions in an ungreased
1-1/2 quart casserole dish. Sprinkle with one cup cheese and 1/2 cup
bread crumbs. Repeat layers; set aside. In a medium bowl, whisk
together eggs, cream, salt and pepper. Pour evenly over onion mixture.
Melt remaining butter in skillet over medium heat; stir in remaining
bread crumbs. Sauté until crumbs are golden; sprinkle over casserole.
Bake at 350 degrees for 25 minutes. Serves 6 to 8.

When friends & family are visiting, hang a small chalkboard in the
kitchen to let them know what's planned for the day, when dinner
is served or any special snow-day activities that might be fun.

Chicken with Garlic & Rosemary

Denise Mainville
Huber Heights, OH

This roast chicken is one of my favorite recipes that I've made for years. Everyone just loves it!

1/4 c. lemon juice
1/4 c. olive oil
2 cloves garlic, sliced
1 T. dried rosemary

2 T. fresh parsley, chopped
1 t. salt
1/4 t. crushed red pepper
3 to 3-1/2 lb. chicken

Combine all ingredients except chicken; pour over chicken in a roasting pan. Marinate for one hour or longer, turning several times; discard marinade. Bake at 400 degrees for one hour, basting frequently with marinade. Serves 4.

On snowy days, it's so nice to enjoy a classic holiday movie before bedtime. Pop some popcorn, get the kids in their jammies and settle in for some laughter and memory-making.

DINNER
at Grandma's

Bacon, Rice & Tomatoes

Staci Meyers
Ideal, GA

*This is a recipe a dear friend made for me.
Now it's one of my favorite comfort foods.*

1-lb. pkg. bacon, chopped and
   crisply cooked, drippings
   reserved
14-1/2 oz. can stewed tomatoes

1/4 c. water
1 T. sugar
salt and pepper to taste
3 c. cooked rice

Combine bacon, tomatoes, water and sugar in a large skillet over
medium heat; stir well. Add 1/4 to 1/2 cup reserved bacon drippings;
reduce heat to medium-low. Cook for 15 minutes; add salt and pepper.
Cook for an additional 5 minutes; serve over rice. Serves 4 to 6.

An antique shop or flea market is just the place to find lots
of vintage shoe and belt buckles. Shoe buckles make elegant
dinner napkin rings, smaller belt buckles are just right for
napkins that are cocktail size.

Steak & Rice Bake

Laura Strausberger
Roswell, GA

A complete meal your family will love.

1 lb. beef sirloin round steak,
   cut into bite-size pieces
1 c. long-cooking rice, uncooked
3 T. butter
1 onion, chopped

1 green pepper, chopped
2 10-3/4 oz. cans cream of
   mushroom soup
10-1/2 oz. can beef consommé

Brown steak and rice in butter in a skillet over medium heat. Add onion and green pepper; cook an additional 3 to 4 minutes, until onion is tender. Stir in remaining ingredients; mix well and pour into a greased 2-quart casserole dish. Cover and bake at 325 degrees for 1-1/2 hours, stirring after 45 minutes. Serves 6.

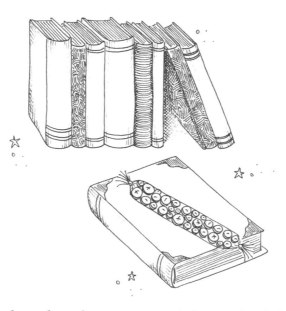

A button bookmark makes a sweet gift for any book lover on your gift list. Stitch buttons of different sizes onto a satin ribbon, then unravel and knot the ends to create a fringe.

Green Bean Bundles

Mary Jo Babiarz
Spring Grove, IL

This recipe is easy to prepare, yet it looks impressive
to serve at a holiday meal.

2 lbs. green beans, trimmed
6 slices bacon, partially cooked
   and halved

garlic salt to taste
1/4 c. butter, melted
3 T. light brown sugar, packed

Steam green beans until crisp-tender. Gather 6 to 10 beans and wrap
1/2 slice of bacon around the center. Repeat with remaining beans;
arrange bundles in lightly greased 13"x9" baking dish. Sprinkle to taste
with garlic salt. Drizzle melted butter over beans; sprinkle with brown
sugar. Bake at 350 degrees for 15 to 20 minutes, or until bacon is
crisp. Serves 6.

Let glowing brown paper lunch sacks lead guests to your
front door. Luminarias are quick to make, simply use holiday
paper punches, available at craft stores, to add cut-outs to
the bags. Open the bag, add sand and nestle in a tealight
or votive inside a votive holder.

Italian Stuffed Chicken

Kathy Solka
Ishpeming, MI

Everyone will think you spent all day in the kitchen!

1 c. sliced mushrooms
2 T. butter
1 c. ricotta cheese
1 c. shredded mozzarella cheese
1/2 c. grated Parmesan cheese

1/2 c. dried parsley
1/4 c. Italian-seasoned dry
   bread crumbs
4 chicken breasts
paprika

In a skillet over medium heat, sauté mushrooms in butter until tender;
set aside. Combine cheeses, parsley and bread crumbs; mix well. Stir
in mushroom mixture. With your fingers, separate skin from chicken
breasts. Spoon mixture underneath skin; sprinkle with paprika.
Arrange chicken in a lightly greased 13"x9" baking pan. Bake at
350 degrees for 30 minutes, or until juice runs clear. Serves 4.

Give your kitchen counter the look of an old-fashioned sweet shoppe!
Collect lots of glass jars, wash thoroughly, then dry and fill with
candy treats for visitors, big and little, to take home.

Golden Potato Pancakes

Gen Mazzitelli
Binghamton, NY

*A super-simple skillet dish that's tasty served
topped with salsa or applesauce.*

4 potatoes, peeled and grated	1 onion, diced
2 c. all-purpose flour	1-1/2 t. salt
2 eggs	1/4 to 1/2 c. oil

Combine potatoes and flour; mix well and set aside. Beat together eggs,
onion and salt in a small mixing bowl. Pour over potatoes; blend well.
Heat 2 tablespoons oil in a large skillet over medium-high heat. Drop
potato mixture by 1/4 cupfuls into skillet. Cook 2 minutes per side, or
until golden. Remove from heat; repeat with remaining potato mixture,
adding oil as needed. Serves 6.

Give a new silver frame an antique look in no time.
Apply brown liquid shoe polish with a cotton rag and rub into
the raised details on the frame. Let the polish dry, then slip
in a sentimental holiday photo.

Turkey & Cranberry Dressing

Barbara Shultis
South Egremont, MA

Your slow cooker does all the work!

8-oz. pkg. stuffing mix
1/2 c. hot water
2 T. butter, softened
1 onion, chopped
1/2 c. celery, chopped
1/4 c. sweetened, dried
   cranberries

3-lb. boneless turkey breast
1/4 t. dried basil
1/2 t. salt
1/2 t. pepper

Place stuffing mix in the bottom of a slow cooker. Add water, butter, onion, celery and cranberries; mix well. Sprinkle turkey with basil, salt and pepper; place on top of stuffing mixture. Cover and cook on low setting for 6 to 7 hours. Remove turkey to a cutting board; stir stuffing until thoroughly mixed. Let turkey and stuffing stand for 5 minutes. Spoon stuffing onto a platter and top with sliced turkey. Serves 4 to 6.

Whip up a cheery pillowcase for special overnight guests...so
easy. Just add a jaunty red trim of rick rack to
a white pillowcase or sham!

Make-Ahead Mashed Potatoes

*Mary Brown
Sayre, PA*

*It's impossible not to love the homestyle flavor
of these potatoes.*

6 to 8 potatoes, peeled and
    quartered
1/4 c. butter, softened

8-oz. pkg. cream cheese,
    softened

Boil potatoes until tender; drain. Combine potatoes, butter and cream cheese in a large bowl; let stand for 10 minutes or until cream cheese melts. Mash until smooth. Refrigerate until serving time; reheat in a microwave. Serves 6.

Even if it isn't snowing, you can have "frost" on the windowpanes.
Follow the manufacturer's instructions on a can of spray frost,
moving your hand from side to side in a gentle sweeping motion
as you spray. Clean up is quick too...simply wipe away
with a paper towel and warm water.

Seafood Lovers' Lasagna

Lisanne Miller
Brandon, MS

I think this tastes even better if made a day ahead,
then reheated so the flavors set in.

32-oz. container ricotta cheese
1 egg, beaten
1 t. Italian seasoning
1 t. garlic, minced
3 6-1/2 oz. cans shrimp,
   drained
3 6-1/2 oz. cans crabmeat,
   drained

16-oz. pkg. frozen corn, thawed
16-oz. pkg. shredded mozzarella
   cheese, divided
2 14-1/2 oz. cans diced
   tomatoes, divided
2 16-oz. pkgs. no-boil lasagna,
   uncooked

Combine ricotta cheese, egg, Italian seasoning, garlic, shrimp, crabmeat, corn, one cup mozzarella and one can diced tomatoes with juices; set aside. Place one layer of lasagna strips in a 13"x9" baking pan that has been coated with non-stick vegetable spray. Spread half the ricotta mixture over lasagna; top with one cup mozzarella and 1/3 cup of remaining diced tomatoes. Repeat layers 2 more times, ending with mozzarella and diced tomatoes. Bake covered at 375 degrees for 30 minutes. Serves 6 to 8.

The answer to anyone's wish for a snowy day...paper snowflakes!
While the kids will happily spend time cutting out dozens of paper
snowflakes, grown-ups will have a ball too! Together with thread
and tape, your family can have their own gentle snowfall anytime!

DINNER
at Grandma's

Garlicky Green Beans

Melanie Lowe
Dover, DE

*Crisp-tender green beans cooked with the flavor
of garlic...a wonderful side for beef dishes.*

3 lbs. green beans, trimmed
1/2 c. olive oil
9 cloves garlic, crushed

1/2 c. fresh parsley, chopped
3/4 c. grated Romano cheese
1 c. dry bread crumbs

Steam green beans until crisp-tender; drain and set aside. Heat oil
in a large skillet; add garlic and parsley. Cook until garlic is lightly
golden; add beans and cook, stirring, for 2 minutes. Remove from
heat; discard garlic. Add cheese and bread crumbs; toss to coat.
Serves 8 to 10.

Christmas waves a magic wand over this world, and behold,
everything is softer and more beautiful.

-Norman Vincent Peale

Sunday Pork Roast

Tiffany Brinkley
Broomfield, CO

Arrange pork slices over mashed potatoes for a farm-style meal that's so hearty and filling.

3 cloves garlic, minced
1 T. dried rosemary
salt and pepper to taste
2 lbs. boneless pork loin roast

1/4 c. olive oil
1/2 c. white wine or chicken broth

Crush garlic with rosemary, salt and pepper. Pierce pork with a sharp knife tip in several places and press half the garlic mixture into openings. Rub pork with remaining garlic mixture and olive oil. Place pork in a lightly greased 13"x9" baking pan. Bake, uncovered, at 350 degrees for 2 hours. Remove to platter; slice and keep warm. Add wine or broth to pan, stirring to loosen browned bits. Serve pan drippings over pork. Serves 8.

A friend who loves scrapbooking will be thrilled to find a gift bag filled with decorative-edged scissors, tags, stickers, buttons, ribbons and rubber stamps.

Aunt Fanny's Baked Squash

Ginger Parsons
Lynchburg, VA

*A flavorful side dish for holiday get-togethers
or church suppers.*

3 lbs. yellow squash, cubed,
   cooked and mashed
1/4 c. butter, softened
2 eggs, beaten
1/2 c. onion, chopped

1 T. sugar
1 t. salt
1/2 t. pepper
3/4 c. bread crumbs, divided
1/4 c. butter, melted

Combine squash, butter, eggs, onion, sugar, salt and pepper; mix well.
Stir in 1/4 cup bread crumbs. Spoon squash mixture into a greased
13"x9" baking pan; set aside. Combine remaining bread crumbs and
melted butter in a small bowl; toss lightly. Sprinkle crumbs over squash
mixture. Bake at 375 degrees for one hour. Serves 8 to 10.

Stencil a galvanized tub with pine trees, stars and moon designs.
Topped with a protective coat of clear acrylic sealer, it's a super gift
filled with kindling, fragrant firestarters and bundles of fatwood.

The Spirit of the Season...
make the holidays extra special for others.

Send a handwritten note to someone who has made a difference in your life.

Drop a coin in an expired parking meter.

Be an elf...secretly leave gifts for a special family.

Donate gently used clothing and toys to a shelter.

Run errands for a friend, neighbor or new mom.

 Deliver cookies to your local fire department.

Shovel the snow from your neighbor's driveway.

Hold the door open for someone else, or give him or her your place in line.

Gather with friends and go caroling at a nursing home.

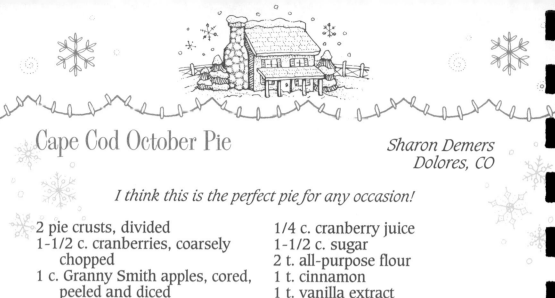

Cape Cod October Pie

Sharon Demers
Dolores, CO

I think this is the perfect pie for any occasion!

2 pie crusts, divided
1-1/2 c. cranberries, coarsely
   chopped
1 c. Granny Smith apples, cored,
   peeled and diced
1/2 c. raisins
1/2 c. chopped walnuts

1/4 c. cranberry juice
1-1/2 c. sugar
2 t. all-purpose flour
1 t. cinnamon
1 t. vanilla extract
4 T. butter, sliced

Line a 9" pie plate with one crust; set aside. Toss together cranberries, apples, raisins, walnuts and cranberry juice; set aside. Combine sugar, flour, cinnamon and vanilla; toss with cranberry mixture. Spoon lightly into prepared pie crust; dot with butter. Cut strips from remaining pie crust; make a lattice over top of pie, sealing to edges. Bake at 425 degrees for about 40 minutes, until fruit is tender and crust is golden. Makes 6 to 8 servings.

Make gourmet cocoa by simply adding a few drops of mint, cinnamon or orange extract and stirring well to blend. So easy!

Gingerbread

Victoria Hoff
Humboldt, NE

It just isn't Christmas without gingerbread.

1 c. brown sugar, packed
1/4 c. butter, melted
2 T. molasses
1 egg, beaten
2 c. all-purpose flour
1 t. baking soda
1 t. salt

1 t. cinnamon
1 t. ground ginger
1/2 t. nutmeg
1/2 t. ground cloves
1 c. sour cream
1 c. raisins

Blend together brown sugar, butter and molasses in a medium bowl; add egg. Mix well; set aside. Sift together flour, baking soda, salt and spices; gradually add to butter mixture. Stir in sour cream and raisins. Place in a greased 9"x5" loaf pan. Bake at 350 degrees for 45 minutes. Cool completely; frost with Brown Sugar Icing. Serves 6 to 8.

Brown Sugar Icing:

1-1/2 c. brown sugar, packed
1/3 c. water

2 T. whipping cream

Combine brown sugar and water in a saucepan over medium heat. Stir mixture until it reaches soft-ball stage, 234 to 243 degrees on a candy thermometer. Remove from heat; beat in cream until smooth.

Kids will love finding surprises tucked into old-fashioned crackers. Just fill a cardboard tube with an assortment of candies, trinkets and confetti. Wrap it all up in colorful paper and tie the ends up with ribbon.

Granny Christian's Biscuit Pudding

Linda Stone
Cookeville, TN

My grandmother, who was born in 1900, made the best biscuit pudding I've ever eaten! After misplacing her recipe for years, and finally retrieving it, I am happy to share it here.

15 frozen biscuits, thawed
3 c. milk
1-1/2 c. water
3 eggs, beaten

1 T. vanilla extract
3/4 c. butter
1/2 c. sugar

Prepare biscuits according to package directions. Cool and crumble; set aside. Mix together remaining ingredients except butter and sugar; add crumbled biscuits. Pour into a lightly greased 13"x9" baking pan. Bake at 350 degrees for 45 minutes; remove from oven and set aside. Melt butter in a saucepan over medium heat; add sugar and cook until sugar is dissolved. Pour over pudding. Serves 10 to 12.

Sugar on snow is a yummy New England treat. Spoon freshly fallen snow into bowls, then drizzle with warm maple syrup. Yum!

Old-Fashioned
SWEETS

Chocolate & Marshmallow Cupcakes
Kathy Grashoff
Fort Wayne, IN

Super for the kids' Christmas parties!

8-oz. pkg. unsweetened dark
    baking chocolate, chopped
1 c. butter, softened
4 eggs
1 c. sugar
3/4 c. all-purpose flour

1 t. salt
1/2 c. mini semi-sweet
    chocolate chips
Garnish: 1/2 c. mini
    marshmallows

Place chocolate and butter together in a microwave-safe bowl; heat on high setting just until melted. Cool slightly, just until warm. Blend together eggs and sugar until light and foamy. Add flour and salt; mix well. Pour in chocolate mixture; blend until smooth. Spoon batter into 12 paper muffin cup liners. Sprinkle one teaspoon chocolate chips over each cupcake. Bake at 350 degrees for 15 minutes, until toothpick tests clean. Remove from oven; arrange several marshmallows on top of each cupcake. Broil just until marshmallows turn golden. Remove from oven and let stand 5 minutes to cool slightly. Makes one dozen.

If you have a windowbox, spruce it up for winter too. Filled with
pine, berries, oranges, apples, nuts and a cranberry garland,
it makes a lovely wintertime welcome.

Vintage Cake

Wendy Lee Paffenroth
Pine Island, NY

This cake is similar to a cake that was mailed to soldiers and sailors during World War II. The flavor is very rich and wonderful.

3-1/2 c. brown sugar, packed and divided
2 T. molasses
1 c. butter
2-1/2 c. all-purpose flour, divided

1 T. vanilla extract, divided
4 eggs, beaten
2 t. baking powder
1-1/2 c. sweetened flaked coconut
2 c. chopped pecans or walnuts

Blend together 1/2 cup brown sugar, molasses, butter, 2 cups flour and one teaspoon vanilla. Spread in a lightly greased 13"x9" baking pan; bake at 350 degrees for 10 minutes. Blend together eggs, remaining vanilla, remaining brown sugar, remaining flour and baking powder. Stir in coconut and nuts until well blended. Spread onto baked crust; bake for an additional 45 minutes. Cool completely; cut into squares. Serves 12 to 15.

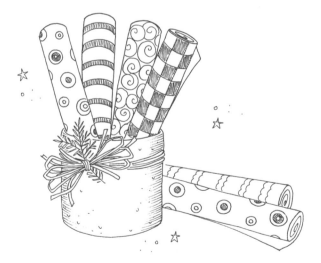

Cover your buffet table with giftwrap...oh-so festive!

Chocolate Chess Pie

Heidi Jo McManaman
Grand Rapids, MI

My favorite winter recipe...Mom always made it at Christmas.

1/2 c. margarine
1-1/2 1-oz. sqs. unsweetened
　　baking chocolate, chopped
1 c. brown sugar, packed
1/2 c. sugar

2 eggs, beaten
1 t. all-purpose flour
1 T. milk
1 t. vanilla extract
9-inch pie crust

Melt butter and chocolate in a small saucepan over low heat; set aside.
Combine sugars, eggs, flour, milk and vanilla in a medium bowl.
Gradually add chocolate mixture, beating constantly. Pour into pie
crust; bake at 325 degrees for 40 to 45 minutes. Let cool before
serving. Serves 6 to 8.

For a gift that's "snow" much fun, fill an enamelware pail with cocoa
mixes, microwave popcorn and a classic holiday video!

Rose Marie's Fruitcake

Rose Marie Rugger
Omaha, NE

*When I wanted a fruitcake with less fruit and more nuts,
I created this recipe.*

1 c. candied pineapple, chopped
1-1/2 c. mixed candied fruit,
  chopped
1 c. chopped dates
2-1/2 c. chopped pecans or
  walnuts
3 c. all-purpose flour, divided

1 c. butter, softened
1 c. sugar
4 eggs
1/4 c. corn syrup
1/4 c. orange juice
1/4 c. sherry or orange juice

Combine fruits and nuts in a large bowl; coat well with one cup flour and set aside. In a large bowl, blend together butter and sugar until light and fluffy. Add eggs, one at a time, beating well after each addition; set aside. Combine corn syrup, orange juice and sherry or orange juice. Add to butter mixture, alternating with remaining flour. Fold in fruits and nuts. Pour batter into eight, greased 5"x3" mini loaf pans. Bake at 275 degrees for 60 to 70 minutes. Makes 8 mini loaves.

Dress up a white frosted cake with beautiful red and green "leaves."
Lightly dust a work surface with sugar and roll red and green
gumdrops until flat. Use a mini leaf-shape cookie cutter
to make leaves. Sweet and simple!

Raisin Bread Pudding & Vanilla Sauce   *Jo Ann*

A slow-cooker version of a classic dessert.

8 slices bread, cubed
4 eggs
2 c. milk
1/2 c. sugar

1/4 c. butter, melted
1/4 c. raisins
1/2 t. cinnamon

Place bread cubes in a greased slow cooker and set aside. Whisk together eggs and milk in a bowl; stir in remaining ingredients. Pour over bread cubes and stir. Cover and cook on high setting for one hour. Reduce setting to low; cook an additional 3 to 4 hours. Serve warm with Vanilla Sauce. Makes 6 servings.

Vanilla Sauce:

2 T. butter
2 T. all-purpose flour
1 c. water

3/4 c. sugar
1 t. vanilla extract

Melt butter in a small saucepan; stir in flour until smooth. Gradually add water, sugar and vanilla. Bring to a boil; cook and stir for 2 minutes, or until thickened. Keep warm.

Pull out the kids' blocks to spell out yuletide greetings. What a nice way to decorate for an open house or progressive dinner.

Apple Gingerbread Cobbler

Wendy Jacobs
Idaho Falls, ID

My new favorite dessert...the flavors are scrumptious!

14-oz. pkg. gingerbread cake
   mix, divided
3/4 c. water
1/4 c. brown sugar, packed

1/2 c. butter, divided
1/2 c. chopped pecans
2 21-oz. cans apple pie filling
Garnish: vanilla ice cream

Mix together 2 cups gingerbread mix and water until smooth; set aside. Stir together remaining gingerbread mix and brown sugar; cut in 1/4 cup butter until mixture is crumbly. Stir in pecans; set aside. Combine pie filling and remaining butter in a large saucepan; cook, stirring often, for 5 minutes over medium heat, or until thoroughly heated. Spoon apple mixture evenly into a lightly greased 11"x7" baking pan. Spoon gingerbread mixture over apple mixture; sprinkle with pecan mixture. Bake at 375 degrees for 30 to 35 minutes, until set. Serve with scoops of ice cream. Serves 8.

Christmas, my child, is love in action.

- Dale Evans

Fudge Cobbler

Sandy Bernards
Valencia, CA

Mmm...what could be better?

1/2 c. butter
1-oz. sq. unsweetened baking
  chocolate
1 c. sugar

1/2 c. all-purpose flour
1 t. vanilla extract
2 eggs, beaten
Garnish: vanilla ice cream

Melt butter and chocolate in a saucepan over low heat, stirring often.
Remove from heat; stir in sugar, flour, vanilla and eggs. Pour batter
into a greased 8"x8" baking pan; bake at 325 degrees for 20 to
22 minutes. Serve warm with ice cream. Serves 9.

Make every Christmas one to remember...take pictures, hold hands,
laugh, sing and make the day nothing short of magical.

Christmas Cherry-Berry Pie

Joyce LaMure
Reno, NV

*The pastry recipe will make enough for two, 2-crust pies...just
freeze the remaining pastry for up to a month.*

21-oz. can cherry pie filling
16-oz. can whole-berry
   cranberry sauce
1/4 c. sugar
3 T. quick-cooking tapioca,
   uncooked

1 t. lemon juice
1/4 t. cinnamon
2 T. butter
1/4 c. milk

Combine all ingredients except butter and milk; let stand 15 minutes.
Divide pastry in half; set one half aside. Roll half the dough out and
line a 9-inch pie plate; add filling. Dot with butter. Roll remaining
dough into a 12-inch circle; cut into 3/4-inch wide strips. Lay strips
on pie at one-inch intervals; fold back alternate strips as you weave
crosswise strips over and under. Trim crust even with outer rim of
pie plate. Dampen edge of crust with water; fold over strips, seal
and crimp. Brush lattice with milk. Bake at 400 degrees for 40 to
45 minutes, covering edge of crust with aluminum foil after
15 minutes to prevent browning. Serves 8.

Flaky Pastry:

3 c. all-purpose flour
1 c. plus 1 T. shortening
1/3 c. cold water

1 egg, beaten
1 T. vinegar
1/2 t. salt

Blend together flour and shortening. Add remaining ingredients; blend
with an electric mixer on low speed.

Forth to the wood did merry men go,
to gather in the mistletoe.

-Sir Walter Scott

Mom's Hot Milk Cake

Linda Maxwell
Staunton, VA

Good served with berries and whipped cream.

1/2 c. butter	1 t. vanilla extract
1 c. milk	2 c. all-purpose flour
4 eggs, beaten	1/2 t. salt
2 c. sugar	1 t. baking powder

Combine butter and milk in a saucepan over medium heat. Bring almost to a boil; set aside. Beat eggs and sugar together; add vanilla, flour and salt. Pour in butter mixture; stir in baking powder and mix well. Spoon into a greased and floured tube pan; bake at 325 degrees for one hour. Cool for 10 minutes; turn out of pan. Serves 12 to 14.

Pull out your button box for oodles of holiday inspiration!
Stitch buttons on mitten cuffs or the edges of woolly scarves.
You can add several to the edges of a tablecloth or string
them together for a country-style garland.

Upside-Down Date Pudding

Beth Cavanaugh
Gooseberry Patch

Try this tasty upside-down version of an old-fashioned dessert.

1 c. chopped dates	1-1/2 c. all-purpose flour
2-1/2 c. boiling water, divided	1 t. baking soda
1/2 c. sugar	1/2 t. baking powder
2 c. brown sugar, firmly packed and divided	1/2 t. salt
	1 c. chopped walnuts
3 T. butter, divided	Garnish: sweetened whipped cream
1 egg	

Combine dates and one cup boiling water in a small bowl; set aside.
Combine sugar, 1/2 cup brown sugar, 2 tablespoons butter and egg
in a large mixing bowl; beat with an electric mixer on medium speed
until blended. Combine flour, baking soda, baking powder and salt in
a separate bowl; stir well. Add to sugar mixture, beating well until a
crumbly mixture forms. Stir in nuts and cooled date mixture. Spoon
batter into a lightly greased 13"x9" baking pan. Combine remaining
brown sugar, remaining boiling water and remaining butter, stirring
well. Pour brown sugar mixture evenly over batter. Bake at
375 degrees for 35 to 40 minutes. Cut into squares and invert onto
serving plates. Serve warm with whipped cream. Makes 12 servings.

Set a plump pillar candle
in a minnow bucket or
an old-fashioned punched
tin lantern for a soft
glow that dances
around the room.

Old-Fashioned
SWEETS

Peanut Butter & Fudge Pudding Cake
Molly Wilson
Rapid City, SD

*Kids big & little are sure to want seconds when you serve this
cake warm with ice cream...yummy!*

1/2 c. all-purpose flour
3/4 c. sugar, divided
3/4 t. baking powder
1/3 c. milk
1 T. oil

1/2 t. vanilla extract
1/4 c. creamy peanut butter
3 T. baking cocoa
1 c. boiling water

Combine flour, 1/4 cup sugar and baking powder in a bowl. Add milk,
oil and vanilla; mix until smooth. Stir in peanut butter; pour into a
lightly greased slow cooker and set aside. Mix together cocoa and
remaining sugar; gradually stir in boiling water. Pour mixture over
batter in slow cooker; do not stir. Cover and cook on high setting for
2 to 3 hours, until a toothpick inserted in the center comes out clean.
Spoon onto serving plates; serve warm. Makes 6 servings.

Keep on the lookout for ice cube trays that make ice cubes
in whimsical shapes...star and pine tree ice cubes would be
such fun floating in punch!

Grandma's Chocolate Cake

Regina Wood
Ava, MO

Grandma always made this when we went to visit at her house.

3 c. all-purpose flour
2 c. sugar
1/3 c. baking cocoa
1/2 t. salt
2 t. baking soda

1 t. vanilla extract
3/4 c. oil
2 T. vinegar
2 c. cold water

Combine all ingredients in order given; mix well. Spread in a greased 13"x9" baking pan. Bake at 350 degrees for 30 to 35 minutes, or until toothpick tests done. Cool completely before spreading with Chocolate Frosting. Serves 12.

Chocolate Frosting:

1/3 c. butter-flavored shortening
1/3 c. baking cocoa
2 c. powdered sugar

1-1/2 t. vanilla extract
2 T. milk

Mix all ingredients together; blend until smooth.

After dinner, linger at the table. Talk about the letters or cards
you've received from friends & family and reminisce
about time spent together.

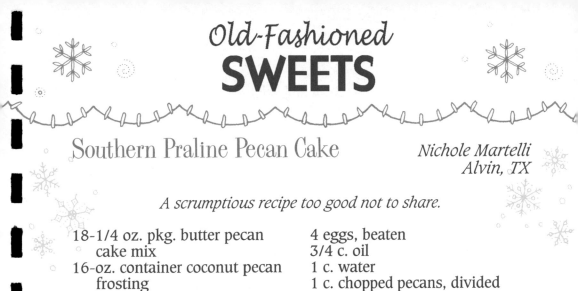

Southern Praline Pecan Cake

Nichole Martelli
Alvin, TX

A scrumptious recipe too good not to share.

18-1/4 oz. pkg. butter pecan
   cake mix
16-oz. container coconut pecan
   frosting

4 eggs, beaten
3/4 c. oil
1 c. water
1 c. chopped pecans, divided

Combine all ingredients except pecans in a large bowl; mix until combined. Stir in half the pecans. Sprinkle remaining pecans in a lightly greased 10" Bundt® pan; pour batter over pecans. Bake at 350 degrees for 50 minutes, or until toothpick inserted near the center comes out clean. Serves 8 to 10.

This year make "real" snow cones...drizzle flavorful fruit juice
over freshly fallen snow!

Poppy Seed Cake

Holly Sutton
Middleburgh, NY

*The glaze drizzled over this simple cake is what makes it stand apart
from other poppy seed cakes.*

18-1/4 oz. pkg. yellow cake mix	1/2 c. sugar
1 c. oil	4 eggs, beaten
1 c. sour cream	1/4 c. poppy seed

Beat together all ingredients; pour into a greased and floured Bundt®
cake pan; bake at 325 degrees for one hour. Spread glaze over the top.
Serves 8 to 10.

Glaze:

1/2 c. sugar	1/2 t. butter extract
1/4 c. orange juice	1/2 t. vanilla extract
1/2 t. almond extract	

Combine all ingredients; mix well.

My idea of Christmas, whether old-fashioned or modern,
is very simple: loving others.

-Bob Hope

Holiday Raisin Cake

Judy Kelly
Saint Charles, MO

My father had a love of raisins that rubbed off on me...this cake is brimming with them! It has a wonderful, spicy flavor, freezes well and is excellent for gift giving.

16-oz. pkg. raisins
2 c. plus 2 t. hot water, divided
1 c. cold water
1/2 c. margarine, sliced
2 c. brown sugar, packed
1 egg, beaten

1 t. ground cloves
1 t. allspice
1 t. nutmeg
2 t. baking soda
4 c. all-purpose flour
1 c. pecans, whole or chopped

In large saucepan, simmer raisins in 2 cups hot water for 15 minutes. Remove from heat and add cold water; stir in margarine, brown sugar, egg and spices. Dissolve baking soda in remaining hot water and stir into raisin mixture along with flour. Mix well; fold in nuts. Pour into a greased angel food or fluted tube pan. Bake at 350 degrees for one hour, or until done. Makes 8 to 10 servings.

Serving up ice cream for dessert? Make it extra special by dipping the rims of dessert bowls in melted chocolate and then immediately dipping them again in chopped nuts or colorful sprinkles. Refrigerate until firm, then fill the bowls with ice cream.

Cranberry Swirl Cake

Mariah Thompson
Smyrna, GA

So refreshingly different from other cakes, this recipe has always been a must-have of mine.

1 c. sugar
1/2 c. butter
2 eggs
2 c. flour
1 t. baking powder
1 t. baking soda

1/2 t. salt
1 c. sour cream
1 t. almond extract
8-oz. can whole-berry cranberry
   sauce
1/2 c. chopped nuts

Gradually beat sugar into butter; stir in eggs, one at a time. In a separate bowl, mix together dry ingredients; stir into egg mixture alternately with sour cream. Add extract. Spoon half the batter into a greased and floured tube pan; spread with cranberry sauce and top with remaining batter. Sprinkle with nuts. Bake at 350 degrees for 50 to 55 minutes. Cool for 5 minutes. Remove from pan; cool completely. Serves 8 to 10.

Trace little hands on cardstock for the sweetest gift tags.

Mom's Vinegar Pie

Regina Penner
El Reno, OK

This pie was a favorite of my Grandmother's in the early 1930's.
Truly handed-down and time-tested, the recipe has now
been passed on to me by my mom and my aunt.

1/4 c. all-purpose flour
1 c. sugar
1 c. boiling water
1 egg, beaten
1 t. lemon extract

3 T. cider vinegar
1 t. nutmeg
1/2 t. salt
9-inch pie crust, baked
Garnish: whipped cream

Mix together all ingredients except crust and whipped cream in a
saucepan; cook over medium-low heat for 5 minutes. Pour filling into
pie crust; cool and top with whipped cream. Serves 8.

A caroling party is a great time for everyone...don't worry if you
sing off key, you'll be terrific! It's all about getting together
with friends and sharing the spirit of the season.

Caramel Rice Pudding

Tyson Ann Trecannelli
Fishing Creek, MD

For a flavor change, use dried cherries or apricots instead of cranberries for this pudding.

14-oz. can sweetened condensed milk
12-oz. can evaporated milk
1 t. vanilla extract
3 c. cooked rice

1/2 to 2/3 c. sweetened, dried cranberries
1 T. brown sugar, packed
1 t. cinnamon

In a medium bowl, mix all ingredients except brown sugar and cinnamon. Spoon into a slow cooker that has been sprayed with non-stick vegetable spray. Cover and cook on low setting for 3 to 4 hours, until liquid is absorbed. Before serving, stir pudding; sprinkle with brown sugar and cinnamon. Serve warm. Makes 8 servings.

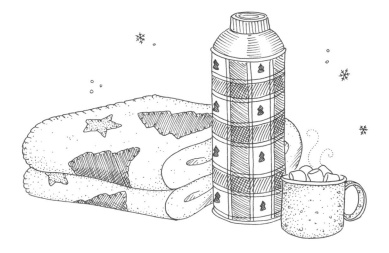

When heading out for wintertime fun, bring extras...spare mittens, socks and sweaters and hats to replace wet ones. And don't forget a thermos of chocolatey cocoa and extra blankets for keeping warm & cozy.

Old-Fashioned
SWEETS

Blue Pan Cranberry Cake

Karen Urfer
New Philadelphia, OH

*A warm, country-style cake I always bake
in a blue spongeware pie pan.*

1 c. cranberries
3/4 c. sugar, divided
1/4 c. chopped walnuts
1 egg

1/2 c. all-purpose flour
1/4 c. plus 2 T. butter, melted
Garnish: whipped cream or
   ice cream

Spread cranberries over the bottom of a greased 9" pie plate. Sprinkle cranberries with 1/4 cup sugar and walnuts; set aside. Beat egg well; add remaining sugar and mix well. Add flour and melted butter; beat well and pour over cranberries. Bake at 325 degrees for 40 to 45 minutes, until golden on top. Serve with whipped cream or ice cream. Serves 8.

Slip napkins and silverware inside a festive mitten and enjoy
dessert outside around a winter's campfire!

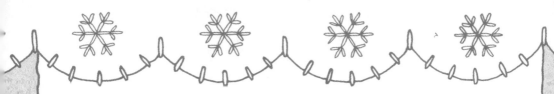

Holiday Must-See Movies...
settle in to enjoy some tried & true classics.

It's a Wonderful Life

Miracle on 34th Street

A Christmas Carol

White Christmas

Christmas in Connecticut

A Charlie Brown Christmas

Rudolph the Red-Nosed Reindeer

Santa Claus is Coming to Town

The Year Without a Santa Claus

Frosty the Snowman

How the Grinch Stole Christmas

Christmas
COOKIE
Exchange

Santa's Favorite Cake Mix Cookies

Kim Conner
South Boston, VA

*A favorite recipe that's so easy...use any flavor of
cake mix for tasty results.*

18-1/4 oz. pkg. red velvet
   cake mix
1/2 c. oil
2 T. water

2 eggs
12-oz. pkg. white chocolate
   chips

Combine all ingredients; mix well. Drop by tablespoonfuls onto lightly
greased baking sheets. Bake at 350 degrees for 8 to 10 minutes. Cool
slightly before removing from baking sheets. Makes 3 dozen.

Remember some cookies ship better than others...chocolate chip,
snickerdoodles, oatmeal and brownies don't break easily;
making them ideal for travel.

Holly Cookies

Flo Burtnett
Gage, OK

Santa will love these...better leave plenty!

2 c. all-purpose flour
1 c. sugar
3/4 t. baking powder
1/4 t. salt
1 t. cinnamon
1/2 c. margarine
1 egg, beaten

1/4 c. milk plus 3 T. milk,
   divided
2/3 c. red plum jam
2 c. powdered sugar
1/2 t. vanilla extract
red cinnamon candies
green food coloring

Combine flour, sugar, baking powder, salt and cinnamon. Cut in margarine until pieces are the size of peas; set aside. Mix egg and 1/4 cup milk; add to flour mixture and stir until moistened. Roll out on a floured surface to 1/8-inch thick. Cut out circles with a 2-inch cookie cutter; place on ungreased baking sheets. Bake at 375 degrees for 8 to 10 minutes; cool. Spread 1/2 teaspoon jam on the bottom of one cookie; top with another. Repeat with remaining cookies; set aside. Blend powdered sugar, vanilla and enough of remaining milk to make a glaze consistency; spread over the top of each cookie. Arrange 2 to 3 cinnamon candies on the top of each; allow glaze to dry. Using a very small paint brush, paint holly leaves and a stem on each cookie with green food coloring. Makes about 4 dozen.

Flea-market finds like vintage pie plates, jelly or canning jars, enamelware pails and retro lunchboxes are sure to bring a smile when filled with holiday sweets!

Butterscotch Gingerbread Cookies

Amy Butcher
Columbus, GA

*These cut-out cookies are my mother's recipe. I loved them as a child,
and now my children love them too. They're so good,
I usually double the recipe!*

1/2 c. butter, softened
1/2 c. brown sugar, packed
3.4-oz. pkg. cook & serve
   butterscotch pudding mix
1 egg, beaten

1-1/2 c. all-purpose flour
1/2 t. baking soda
1-1/2 t. ground ginger
1 t. cinnamon

Blend together butter, brown sugar and pudding mix; add egg. Mix in
remaining ingredients. Chill for 30 minutes. Roll out 1/4-inch thick
on a floured surface; cut with cookie cutters as desired. Arrange on
greased baking sheets and bake for 8 to 10 minutes at 350 degrees.
Makes about one dozen.

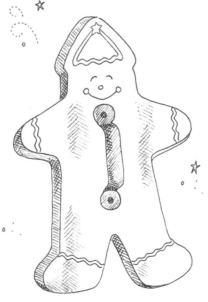

Edible glitter and sparkling sanding sugar make candy,
cookies and brownies look absolutely magical.

Grandma Hazel's Sugar Cookies

Lynne McKaige
Savage, MN

My grandma had quite a sweet tooth! You'll find that these cookies melt in your mouth.

1 c. margarine, softened	1/2 t. baking soda
1 c. sugar	1 t. cider vinegar
1-1/2 c. all-purpose flour	1 t. vanilla extract

Blend together margarine and sugar. Add remaining ingredients; mix well. Refrigerate dough for 30 minutes. Roll dough into one-inch balls; arrange at least 2 inches apart on ungreased baking sheets. Bake at 300 degrees for 18 to 20 minutes. Remove to a wire rack to cool. Makes 2 to 3 dozen.

Homebaked cookies are always appreciated. Pack them in cello bags tied up with rick rack and set in a basket near the door...guests will love choosing a bag to take home with them.

Coconut-Almond Fudge Bars

Linda Nichols
Wintersville, OH

Oh-so rich and good!

18-1/2 oz. pkg. fudge cake mix
16-oz. container coconut-
   almond frosting

1 c. applesauce
1 egg, beaten

Mix together all ingredients; spread in a lightly greased 13"x9" baking pan. Bake at 350 degrees for 30 to 32 minutes, until toothpick tests clean; cool for 15 minutes. To serve, cut into 2-inch squares. Makes about 2 dozen.

If your cookie recipe calls for a cookie press and you don't
have one, go to the cupboard and begin turning over glasses!
You'll find some with the prettiest designs. Simply dip them
in sugar before pressing on balls of dough.

Salted Nut Roll Bars

Sandy Groezinger
Stockton, IL

A yummy recipe that's ideal for holiday open houses or cookie swaps.

18-1/2 oz. pkg. yellow cake mix
3/4 c. butter, melted and divided
1 egg, beaten
3 c. mini marshmallows
10-oz. pkg. peanut butter chips

1/2 c. light corn syrup
1 t. vanilla extract
2 c. salted peanuts
2 c. crispy rice cereal

Combine cake mix, 1/4 cup butter and egg; press into a greased 13"x9" baking pan. Bake at 350 degrees for 10 to 12 minutes. Sprinkle marshmallows over baked crust; return to oven and bake for 3 additional minutes, or until marshmallows are melted. In a saucepan over medium heat, melt peanut butter chips, corn syrup, remaining butter and vanilla. Stir in nuts and cereal. Spread mixture over marshmallow layer. Chill briefly until firm; cut into squares. Makes 2-1/2 dozen bars.

Dress up any cookie by simply dipping the edges in melted chocolate, peanut butter or butterscotch chips.

Chocolate Sandwich Cookies

Kristie Rigo
Friedens, PA

These cookies are great right away, but even better
a day or 2 later...if you can wait!

2 18-1/4 oz. pkgs. devil's food   4 eggs, beaten
   cake mix   2/3 c. oil

Beat together cake mixes, eggs and oil; dough will be very stiff. Roll
into one-inch balls; arrange on ungreased baking sheets. Flatten balls
slightly; bake at 350 degrees for 8 to 10 minutes. Cool on baking
sheets for 3 minutes; remove to wire rack. Spread icing on the bottom
of a cookie; place another cookie on top. Repeat with remaining
cookies and icing. Makes 4 dozen.

Icing:

1 c. milk   1/2 c. shortening
5 T. all-purpose flour   1 c. sugar
1/2 c. butter, softened   1 t. vanilla extract

Combine milk and flour in a saucepan over medium heat; cook and stir
until thick. Cover and refrigerate. In a separate bowl, beat together
butter, shortening, sugar and vanilla until creamy. Add chilled milk
mixture; beat for 10 minutes with an electric mixer on medium speed.

Few sights are more charming than that of a town covered with
new-fallen, clean, white snow; and how pretty it is to watch the tiny
flakes drift downward through the air, as if there were a wedding
in the sky and the fairies were throwing confetti.

- Cyril W. Beaumont

Washtub Cookies

Joyce LaMure
Reno, NV

The fun name comes from the fact that with all the ingredients,
you just might need a washtub big enough to mix them all up in!
Get out your biggest mixing bowl...you're going to need it!

1 c. shortening
1/2 c. butter
2 c. sugar
1-3/4 c. brown sugar, packed
1/3 c. molasses
4 eggs, beaten
2 t. vanilla extract
1 c. crunchy peanut butter
3 c. all-purpose flour

6 c. quick-cooking oats,
  uncooked
2 t. baking soda
1 t. salt
2 t. cinnamon
1/2 t. nutmeg
1/2 t. ground ginger
1/2 t. allspice
1-1/2 c. peanuts, chopped

Combine shortening, butter, sugar, brown sugar, molasses, eggs, vanilla and peanut butter together in a very large mixing bowl. Beat just until blended; set aside. In another very large bowl, combine remaining ingredients; add to shortening mixture. Mix until well blended. Drop by tablespoonfuls, 2 inches apart, onto lightly greased baking sheets. Bake at 350 degrees for 8 to 10 minutes; cool on wire rack. Makes 6 dozen.

For a yummy change when making powdered sugar icing, instead of milk, use half-and-half and a squeeze of lemon juice.

Mrs. Claus' Shortbread Cookies

Gail Collins
Woodstock, MD

These are the most delicious shortbread cookies I've ever tasted!

1 c. super-fine sugar
1-lb. pkg. butter, softened
4 c. all-purpose flour

Optional: semi-sweet chocolate
chips, melted

Blend sugar, butter and flour until well mixed. Spread in a greased 13"x9" baking pan. Place a length of wax paper over top and press dough down. Remove paper; pierce dough all over with a fork. Bake at 325 degrees for 30 minutes. Immediately cut into bars; let cool. If desired, dip half of each cookie into melted chocolate; set on wax paper to dry. Store in an airtight container. Makes 2 dozen.

Cookies make scrumptious placecards when you pipe
on guests' names with frosting!

Tiramisu Cookie Log

Lori Brooks
Cumming, GA

This no-bake treat is so easy to whip up!

1 pt. whipping cream
sugar to taste
15-oz. pkg. chocolate chip
    cookies

2 c. brewed espresso or strong
    coffee, cooled
Garnish: mini semi-sweet
    chocolate chips

Using an electric mixer on medium-high speed, beat together whipping cream and sugar until stiff; set aside. Quickly dip 2 cookies into cooled coffee. Using a dab of whipped cream, sandwich cookies together upright, creating a log. Repeat process until desired length of log is reached. When finished, cover log with remaining whipped cream; garnish with mini chocolate chips. Chill until ready to serve, no more than 3 to 4 hours. Serves about 10.

Use jelly-roll pans or baking sheets with sides only for
bar cookies...drop or slice & bake cookies won't
bake evenly in a pan with sides.

Minty Cheesecake Bars

Jo Ann

*Yummy mint and chocolate together...be prepared
to share the recipe.*

4 1-oz. sqs. unsweeted baking
    chocolate, coarsely chopped
1/2 c. plus 2 T. butter, divided
2 c. sugar
4 eggs, divided
2 t. vanilla extract
1 c. all-purpose flour
8-oz. pkg. cream cheese,
    softened

1 T. cornstarch
14-oz. can sweetened condensed
    milk
1 t. peppermint extract
Optional: green food coloring
1 c. semi-sweet chocolate chips
1/2 c. whipping cream
Garnish: crushed peppermints

Melt baking chocolate with 1/2 cup butter; stir until smooth. Combine
chocolate mixture with sugar, 3 eggs, vanilla and flour in a large
bowl, blending well. Spread in a greased 13"x9" baking pan. Bake
for 12 minutes at 350 degrees. Beat together cream cheese, remaining
butter and cornstarch in a medium bowl until fluffy. Gradually beat in
condensed milk, remaining egg, extract and food coloring, if desired.
Pour mixture over hot chocolate layer; bake for 30 minutes, or until
set. Combine chocolate chips and cream in a small saucepan. Cook
over low heat until smooth, stirring constantly. Spread over mint layer;
sprinkle with crushed peppermints and let cool. Refrigerate until set;
cut into bars. Store covered in refrigerator. Makes 2 to 3 dozen bars.

Santa will love this eggnog punch! Combine 2 pints of softened
peppermint ice cream with one cup of ginger ale
and one quart of eggnog.

Noel Bars

Carol Barnes
East Greenville, PA

So pretty...they look like they've been dusted with snow.

2/3 c. all-purpose flour	4 eggs
2 c. brown sugar, packed	2 t. vanilla extract
1/4 t. baking soda	1/4 c. butter, melted
1/4 t. salt	Garnish: powdered sugar
1 c. chopped walnuts	

Combine flour, brown sugar, baking soda, salt and walnuts; set aside.
Beat together eggs and vanilla in a small bowl; add to dry mixture,
mixing well. Spread butter in a 8"x8" baking pan; pour batter over top.
Bake at 350 degrees for 20 minutes; cool. Cut into squares and
sprinkle with powdered sugar. Serves 16.

Quick & Easy Lemon Bars

Lynda McCormick
Burkburnett, TX

Simple to make...a holiday must-have.

16-oz. pkg. one-step angel food	Optional: chopped pecans,
cake mix	flaked coconut
22-oz. can lemon pie filling	

Mix dry cake mix and pie filling in a large bowl. Spread in a greased
15"x10" jelly-roll pan; top with pecans or coconut as desired. Bake at
350 degrees for 30 minutes. Let cool; cut into bars. Makes 2-1/2 dozen.

It's that time of year when it's good to be fat & jolly!

-Unknown

My Kids' Favorite Cookies

Mary Solberg
Jordan, MN

*When my grown children were still at home,
this is the cookie they asked for most often.*

2-1/4 c. all-purpose flour
1/2 c. sugar
1/2 c. brown sugar, packed
1/2 t. baking soda
1/2 t. salt
1/2 t. cinnamon
1/4 t. nutmeg
1 c. shortening

1/2 c. peanut butter
1/4 c. applesauce
1/2 t. vanilla extract
1 egg, beaten
1 c. quick-cooking oats,
   uncooked
Garnish: 1/4 c. favorite-flavored
   jelly or jam

Combine all ingredients except for jelly or jam; mix well. Form into
one-inch balls; place on a baking sheet. Flatten with a fork; place
1/8 teaspoon jelly in the center of each cookie. Bake at 350 degrees for
12 to 14 minutes. Makes 5 dozen.

Make cookie giving fun...tuck lots of wrapped cookies inside
a big Christmas stocking!

Christmas
COOKIE EXCHANGE

Gumdrop Cookies

Celeste Reszel
Des Moines, IA

A recipe belonging to my great-grandmother...I remember when we came to visit, she always had them tucked away in her freezer.

1 c. sugar
1/2 c. brown sugar, packed
1 c. shortening
2 eggs, beaten
1 t. vanilla extract

2-1/3 c. all-purpose flour
1 t. salt
1 t. baking soda
1 c. gumdrops, chopped
Optional: 1/2 c. chopped nuts

Mix together sugar, brown sugar, shortening, eggs and vanilla. Gradually add dry ingredients. Add gumdrops and nuts, if using; mix well. Drop by rounded teaspoonfuls onto ungreased baking sheets. Bake at 350 degrees for 15 minutes. Makes about 5 dozen.

Write your holiday greetings on a length of twill tape using fabric paint. When the paint has dried, use it as a whimsical ribbon to wrap up any gift.

Mom's Soft Italian Cookies

Helene Santia
Upland, CA

Sometimes I add a bit of food coloring to the glaze
for a festive look.

1 c. margarine, softened
8 eggs, beaten
1-1/2 c. sugar

1 T. vanilla extract
5 T. baking powder
5 c. all-purpose flour

Blend together margarine, eggs and sugar; mix well. Stir in vanilla and baking powder. Gradually add flour to margarine mixture. Drop dough by rounded tablespoonfuls onto ungreased baking sheets. Bake at 400 for 10 to 12 minutes, until golden; cool for 10 minutes. Drizzle with Glaze. Makes 6 dozen.

Glaze:

1 c. powdered sugar
1 to 2 T. milk

1/2 t. vanilla, anise or lemon
    extract

Mix together all ingredients until smooth.

White buttons arranged in the shape of a snowflake are
so charming glued onto a wrapped gift.

Sugar Diamonds

Debi DeVore
Dover, OH

Just scrumptious!

1 c. butter, softened
1 c. sugar
1 egg, separated
1/2 t. vanilla extract

2 c. all-purpose flour
1/2 t. cinnamon
1/8 t. salt
1/2 c. chopped pecans

Blend butter and sugar. Add egg yolk and vanilla; mix well and set aside. Combine flour, cinnamon and salt; gradually add to butter mixture. Spread dough in a greased 15"x10" jelly-roll pan. Cover with plastic wrap and press evenly into pan; remove wrap and set aside. Beat egg white until frothy; brush over dough. Sprinkle with pecans. Bake at 300 degrees for 30 minutes. Cut into 1-1/2 inch diamond shapes while still warm. Makes about 6 dozen.

Cookies can be given in lots of clever ways. Wrapped up in
a tea towel, they can be tucked into a vintage flour sifter,
a retro cookie jar or nestled inside a child's sand pail.

Coconut Christmas Bites

Kathy Grashoff
Fort Wayne, IN

Bite-size treats...you can't stop at one!

1/3 c. butter, melted
1 c. graham cracker crumbs
14-oz. can sweetened condensed milk
6-oz. pkg. sweetened flaked coconut
2 c. chopped pecans

1 c. chopped dates
1/2 c. candied cherries, chopped
1/2 c. candied pineapple, chopped
1 t. vanilla extract
1 t. almond extract

Combine butter and cracker crumbs; add remaining ingredients. Mix well; spoon by tablespoonfuls into paper-lined mini muffin cups. Bake at 325 degrees for 25 to 30 minutes. Remove from pans; cool completely on wire racks. Makes 6 dozen.

Family photos make the best gift tags. Copy, cut out, hole punch and tie on...you get the package with your picture on it!

Butter-Nut Snowballs

Paula Bondy
White Lake, MI

*I first made these cookies with my friend, Linda, at Christmastime
in 1987. Now, every time I make them, I think of her
and the great fun we had that day.*

1 c. butter, softened
1/2 c. sugar
2 t. vanilla extract
2 c. all-purpose flour

1/2 t. salt
2 c. pecans, finely chopped
Garnish: powdered sugar

Mix together butter, sugar and vanilla until light and fluffy; set aside.
In a separate bowl, combine flour and salt; add to butter mixture,
blending thoroughly. Stir in pecans. Form into one-inch balls; arrange
on lightly greased baking sheets. Bake at 325 degrees for about
15 to 20 minutes, until set but not brown. Cool; roll into powdered
sugar. Makes 6 dozen.

Fill a Santa hat with wrapped cookies and set at each
table setting...a yummy take-home gift!

Forgotten Cookies

Audrey Galpin
Upper Black Edy, PA

*I usually make these cookies after dinner
and leave them in the oven overnight.*

2 egg whites at room temperature
1/4 t. salt
3/4 c. sugar

1 t. vanilla extract
6-oz. pkg. semi-sweet chocolate
chips

Preheat oven to 375 degrees. Beat together egg whites and salt with
an electric mixer on medium speed until frothy. Gradually add sugar,
beating until soft peaks form. Stir in vanilla; fold in chocolate chips.
Drop by teaspoonfuls onto greased baking sheets. Place cookies in
oven; turn off oven. Leave cookies in oven for 6 to 8 hours. Makes
2-1/2 dozen.

A gardening friend will be tickled to find your best homebaked
goodies inside a new terra cotta pot! Turn the saucer
upside down and place over the opening of the pot,
then secure the "lid" with a plump bow.

Cinnamon Gingersnaps

Lisa Ashton
Aston, PA

So nice for dipping into a cup of herbal tea.

3/4 c. butter, softened	2 t. baking soda
1 c. brown sugar, packed	2 t. cinnamon
1 egg, beaten	1 t. ground ginger
1/4 c. molasses	1/2 t. salt
2-1/4 c. all-purpose flour	1/2 to 1 c. sugar

Blend together butter and brown sugar in a large bowl. Add egg and molasses; set aside. Combine flour, baking soda, cinnamon, ginger and salt in a separate large bowl. Gradually add flour mixture to butter mixture; mix well. Roll dough into one-inch balls; roll in sugar. Arrange on ungreased baking sheets 2 inches apart. Bake at 350 degrees for 10 to 12 minutes, or until cookies are set and tops are cracked. Remove to wire rack. Makes 4 dozen.

A Christmas family-party! We know nothing in nature more delightful! There seems a magic in the very name of Christmas.

- Charles Dickens

Ho-Ho-Holiday Spritz

Geneva Rogers
Gillette, WY

Oh-so pretty!

2/3 c. sugar
1 c. butter, softened
1 egg
1/2 t. salt

1 t. nutmeg
2 t. vanilla extract
2-1/4 c. all-purpose flour

Combine all ingredient except flour in a large mixing bowl. With an electric mixer on medium speed, beat until mixture is light and fluffy, 2 to 3 minutes. Add flour; beat at low speed until well mixed, about 2 to 3 minutes. If dough is too soft, cover and refrigerate until firm, 30 to 45 minutes. Place dough into a cookie press. Form desired shapes one inch apart on ungreased baking sheets. Bake at 400 degrees for 6 to 8 minutes, or until edges are lightly golden. Drizzle warm cookies with glaze. Makes 4 dozen.

Glaze:

1 c. powdered sugar
1/4 c. butter, softened

2 T. water
1/4 t. rum extract

Mix together all ingredients; stir until smooth.

Snowflake Press Cookies

Liz Hall
Worthington, IN

Dust baked cookies with sanding sugar for sparkle!

1/2 c. butter, softened	1 t. vanilla extract
1/2 c. shortening	1 t. orange zest
3-oz. pkg. cream cheese, softened	2-1/2 c. all-purpose flour
1 c. sugar	1/2 t. salt
1 egg yolk	1/4 t. cinnamon

Blend butter, shortening and cream cheese; add sugar, egg yolk, vanilla and orange zest. Mix well; set aside. Combine flour, salt and cinnamon; stir into butter mixture. Chill for 30 minutes; place dough into a cookie press. Form snowflakes one inch apart on ungreased baking sheets. Bake at 350 degrees for 12 to 15 minutes. Makes 4 dozen.

Get the family together for a photo with Santa...sure to make big and little kids giggle!

No-Bake Fruitcake Slices

Amy Buell
Cumberland Gap, TN

These super-easy cookies are always a nice hostess gift.

16-oz. pkg. vanilla wafers,
  finely crushed
1 c. red candied cherries,
  chopped
1 c. green candied cherries,
  chopped

1 c. candied pineapple, chopped
2 c. English walnuts, chopped
14-oz. can sweetened condensed
  milk
2 T. whiskey or vanilla extract
Garnish: powdered sugar

Mix all ingredients except powdered sugar together in a large mixing
bowl. Divide into 4 portions; form each into an 8-inch by 2-inch
roll. Coat each roll in powdered sugar; wrap with wax or parchment
paper and twist ends. Chill; cut into 1/2-inch to one-inch slices. Keep
refrigerated. Makes about 3 dozen.

Toasted nuts are oh-so simple to make and give cookies such
flavor. Give it a try...just spread nuts on a baking pan and
bake for 5 to 10 minutes in a 350-degree oven until golden.

Candy Cane Twists

Elizabeth Blackstone
Racine, WI

Absolutely perfect for Christmas!

1/2 c. peppermint candies, crushed	1 egg, beaten
1/2 c. sugar	1 t. vanilla extract
1/2 c. butter, softened	1/2 t. peppermint extract
1/2 c. shortening	2-1/2 c. all-purpose flour
1 c. powdered sugar	1/2 t. red food coloring

Mix crushed candies and sugar in a small bowl; set aside. Combine butter, shortening, powdered sugar, egg and extracts in a large bowl. Beat with an electric mixer on medium-high speed until light and fluffy, 2 to 3 minutes. Reduce mixer to medium-low speed; gradually add flour, mixing just until blended. Divide dough into 2 bowls; stir red food coloring into one. For each cookie, roll one teaspoonful plain dough and one teaspoonful red dough between hands to form two, 4-inch ropes. Twist ropes together and shape into a candy cane. Arrange one inch apart on ungreased baking sheets. Bake at 375 degrees for 8 to 10 minutes, until firm and light golden, moving baking sheets from upper to lower rack midway through baking time. Immediately sprinkle cookies with peppermint mixture; transfer to wire racks to cool. Makes 4 dozen.

When making a gingerbread house, deck it with
snowy "pine" trees...rosemary sprigs brushed
with corn syrup, then dusted with sugar!

Sweet Butter Cookies

Linda Bollinger
Erie, PA

*Also known as Vinegar Cookies, these have been a favorite
in our family for many years...it's hard to eat just one!
They are quick & easy to make, and no eggs are needed.*

1 c. butter, softened	2 t. white vinegar
3/4 c. sugar	1-3/4 c. all-purpose flour
1 t. baking soda	1 t. vanilla extract

Blend together butter and sugar until creamy. Add baking soda and
vinegar; mix. Stir in flour; add vanilla. Drop by teaspoonfuls onto
ungreased baking sheets. Bake at 350 degrees for 12 to 15 minutes,
until light golden. Makes 4 to 5 dozen.

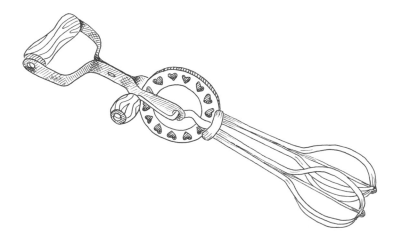

Need softened butter in a jiffy? Grate sticks with a cheese grater
and it will soften in just minutes!

Gram's Christmas Crescents

Connie Lombardi
Camden, NY

When I was a little girl, I went to my great-grandma's house in the summer with my cousin, Charrise. We would sit on Gram's porch for hours and shell butternuts. When we thought we would never finish, we remembered just what Gram was going to do with all those butternuts. I can still see Gram with her apron on, rocking in her rocker, shelling butternuts.

1 c. butter, softened
2 c. all-purpose flour
1 t. vanilla extract

1 c. butternuts or walnuts,
  chopped
1/4 c. powdered sugar

Work together butter, flour and vanilla until mixture resembles pie dough; add nuts. Form one-inch balls into crescents; place on ungreased baking sheets. Bake at 350 degrees for 8 to 10 minutes. Let cool on wire rack. Place powdered sugar in a plastic zipping bag and shake cooled cookies in the sugar. Makes 4 dozen.

May our house be too small to hold all of our friends.

- Traditional toast

Pecan Sugar Cookies

Michelle Rogde
Mokena, IL

While I was growing up, my grandmother lived with us. Together we would make Christmas cookies. This recipe is one of our favorites!

1 c. butter, softened	2 c. all-purpose flour
3/4 c. brown sugar, packed	Garnish: red and green colored
1 t. vanilla extract	sugar, pecan halves

Blend together butter and brown sugar until fluffy; add vanilla. Gradually add flour and mix thoroughly. Chill for one hour. Form dough into one-inch balls; roll in colored sugar. Arrange on ungreased baking sheets; flatten with a glass until about 1/2-inch thick. Press a pecan half into center. Bake at 325 degrees for 10 to 12 minutes. Makes about 4 dozen.

Make a Hug-in-a-Mug gift for a co-worker. Fill an oversize mug
with packages of cocoa mix and candy canes for stirring.
Given with a stack of homebaked cookies tied up
with a bow, they're sure to be welcome surprise.

Chocolate Mint Chippers

Vickie

*These cookies crisp up as they cool. If you like a softer cookie,
bake them for just 10 to 12 minutes.*

3/4 c. butter-flavored shortening
1/2 c. sugar
1/2 c. brown sugar, packed
1 egg
1 t. vanilla extract
1 t. peppermint extract

2 to 2-1/4 c. all-purpose flour
1/4 c. baking cocoa
1 t. baking soda
1/4 t. salt
1 c. semi-sweet chocolate chips

Blend together butter, sugar and brown sugar in a large bowl until
light and fluffy. Beat in egg. Stir in extracts; set aside. Combine flour,
cocoa, baking soda and salt; gradually stir into butter mixture. Stir in
chocolate chips. Drop by tablespoonfuls onto lightly greased baking
sheets. Bake at 350 degrees for 12 to 15 minutes. Cool on baking
sheets for 5 minutes before removing to wire rack. Makes about
2-1/2 dozen.

To keep freshly baked cookies from sticking together, give them
plenty of time to cool before packing them up.

Snow-Covered Macadamia Treats

Deborah Byrne
Clinton, CT

Every year at Christmas I make 15 different kinds of cookies and candies to give as gifts...these treats are the most popular.

1/2 c. sugar
1 c. butter, softened
1-1/2 t. vanilla extract
2 c. all-purpose flour

1/2 c. white chocolate chips
1/2 c. macadamia nuts, chopped
2 T. powdered sugar

Combine sugar, butter and vanilla in a large bowl; blend until light and fluffy. Add flour; mix well. Stir in chocolate chips and nuts. With floured hands, form rounded teaspoonfuls into 2-inch logs. Place 2 inches apart on ungreased baking sheets. Bake at 350 degrees for 10 to 12 minutes, or until firm to the touch. Let cool for one minute; remove to wire racks and let cool. Sprinkle lightly with powdered sugar. Makes 3 dozen.

Slip jingle bells onto wire, then twist into cheery napkin rings...a holly jolly jingle for your neighborhood cookie swap!

Chocolate-Covered Cherry Cups

Robin Healy
Honeoye, NY

*I created this simpler version of a more difficult recipe and
I think they tuned out wonderful! My grandchildren like
to push the cherries in for me.*

20-oz. pkg. brownie mix
16-oz. jar maraschino cherries,
   drained, 1/2 c. juice reserved
   and divided

6-oz. pkg. semi-sweet chocolate
   chips
1/2 c. sweetened condensed
   milk

Prepare brownie batter according to package directions, using 1/4 cup
cherry juice plus water needed to equal amount of liquid called for.
Place paper liners in mini muffin cups; fill about 1/2 full of brownie
batter. Push a cherry into each cup; bake at 350 degrees for 15 to
20 minutes. Remove baked cups in liners from muffin cups; let cool.
Combine chocolate chips and condensed milk in a small saucepan; stir
over low heat until melted. Remove from heat; stir in remaining cherry
juice as needed for frosting consistency. Place a dollop of warm frosting
on each cherry cup. Let cool. Makes 3 dozen.

Send cookies to college students so they arrive just before
final exams...a sure-fire way to make them smile.

Cookie Swap Success...
sweets with oh-so simple packaging!

Serve up truffles in candy cups and pack flavorful assortments into festive cardboard boxes.

Arrange chocolate-dipped candy canes or pretzels into cello bags, fold over the tops of the bags and staple them closed. Finish off packages with a cheery ribbon and gift tag.

Tie a vintage silver fork onto a package of peanut butter cookies...don't forget the recipe and instructions for making the pretty criss-cross pattern!

Nestle mini cookies inside a pretty teacup and give with a box of herbal tea...a warming go-with for your cookie treats.

Chenille stems make fun, old-fashioned toppers for packaged cookie swap treats! Twist together one red and one white chenille stem, then bend the top over to resemble a candy cane.

Brown kraft paper is a simple, country-style wrap for boxed cookies...add a rick rack bow and it's ready for gift giving!

Cool & Creamy Peppermint Fudge

Vickie

The best...a Christmas must-have for any bake sale.

2 10-oz. pkgs. white chocolate
   chips
14-oz. can sweetened condensed
   milk

1/2 to 1 t. peppermint extract
1-1/2 c. peppermint candy
   canes, crushed
1/4 t. red or green food coloring

Combine chocolate chips and condensed milk in a saucepan over medium heat. Stir frequently until chips are almost melted. Remove from heat; continue to stir until smooth. When chips are completely melted, stir in extract, food coloring and crushed candy. Place aluminum foil in a 8"x8" baking pan. Grease foil and spread chocolate mixture over foil. Chill for 2 hours; cut into squares. Makes about 5 dozen.

Packaging candy is quick & easy when you fill reusable aluminum canisters, available at craft stores. Wrap or tie ribbons around the canisters, using craft glue to hold the ribbons in place. Decorate the lids with tags or stickers, secure the lids and your gift is ready!

Eggnog Fudge

Sue Neitzel
West Plains, MO

A holiday favorite becomes a sweet treat.

3 c. sugar
1 c. eggnog
1-1/2 c. mini marshmallows
1/2 t. cinnamon

1/2 t. nutmeg
2 T. butter
6-oz. pkg. white chocolate chips
1 c. slivered almonds

Combine sugar and eggnog in a large sauccpan. Bring to a rolling boil over medium heat, stirring constantly. Boil for 2 minutes. Fold in marshmallows, cinnamon and nutmeg. Bring back to a rolling boil; cook for 6 minutes, stirring constantly. Remove from heat; stir in butter, chocolate chips and almonds. Stir until well mixed. Pour into a greased aluminum foil-lined 9"x9" baking pan. Cool completely at room temperature. Turn out of pan; peel off aluminum foil and cut into squares. Makes about 5 dozen.

Dress up mixes or candies by tucking them into festive red and white gift bags. A metal-rimmed tag stamped with a holiday greeting and tied on with ribbon makes an easy gift tag.

Reindeer Food

Stephanie Kemp
Millersburg, OH

*When my youngest son, Matthew, was 7, he made this snack mix.
He packaged it in jars for Christmas presents to aunts and
uncles...everyone loves it!*

14-oz. pkg. oat cereal with mini
   marshmallows
10-oz. pkg. tiny pretzels
14-oz. pkg. candy-coated
   chocolates

3-1/2 c. mixed nuts
16-oz. pkg. white melting
   chocolate, chopped

Mix together all ingredients except melting chocolate in a large bowl;
set aside. Melt white chocolate in a microwave-safe bowl on high
setting for one minute, stir, then repeat at 15 second intervals until
melted. Pour over dry ingredients; mix well. Spread onto wax
paper; let stand for about one hour. Store in an airtight container.
Makes 24 cups.

Wrap treats in decorated cellophane sacks...oh-so easy.
Use a paint pen to dress up bags with dots, lines,
greetings and swirls, then tie up with ribbon.

Microwave Caramel Party Mix

Darcy Schuur
Chandler, MN

Super simple, super tasting!

9 c. bite-size crispy rice cereal
   squares
12-oz. pkg. peanuts
1 lb. can mixed nuts
1/4 c. corn syrup
1/2 c. butter
1/2 c. brown sugar, packed
1/4 t. baking soda
1/2 t. vanilla extract
14-oz. pkg. candy-coated
   chocolates

Combine cereal, peanuts and mixed nuts in a brown paper bag; set aside. Mix corn syrup, butter and brown sugar together in a microwave-safe bowl; microwave for 4 minutes on high setting, stirring 3 times. Add baking soda and vanilla; pour over cereal mixture. Shake bag to coat; microwave on high setting for 1-1/2 minutes. Shake to mix; microwave for an additional 15 seconds. Stir in candy; pour onto wax paper. Let set. Makes about 16 cups.

Button-covered boxes are full of whimsy! Use hot glue to attach buttons of different sizes and colors every-which-way on a plain box. Wrap it all up with an airy organdy ribbon...fun!

Zesty Dressing Mix

Melody Taynor
Everett, WA

This Italian dressing mix is a great quick-to-fix gift.

1/4 c. dried oregano
2 T. garlic powder
2 T. onion powder
2 T. dried parsley
2 t. dried basil

1/2 t. dried thyme
1/2 t. celery salt
2 T. sugar
1 T. salt
2 t. pepper

Blend together all ingredients in a small bowl. Place in a half-pint jar; attach instructions. Makes one cup mix.

Instructions:

In a small bowl, whisk together 1/4 cup white vinegar, 2/3 cup oil, 2 tablespoons water and 2 tablespoons dressing mix. Delicious on tossed salads and pasta salads, submarine sandwiches and grilled meats.

Spoon Zesty Dressing Mix into a half-pint canning jar and nestle in a basket. Tuck in breadsticks and a jar of marinara sauce for dipping...what a super hostess gift!

The Christmas
PANTRY

Fiesta Dip Mix

Nicole Herda
Two Rivers, WI

Everyone who has tried this mix loves it! It's excellent in casseroles or on meat, and it makes a great little gift, too.

1/2 c. dried parsley
1/3 c. dried, minced onion
1/3 c. chili powder

1/4 c. dried chives
1/4 c. dried cumin
1/4 c. salt

Combine all ingredients in a pint jar; cover tightly and attach instructions. Makes about 2 cups mix.

Instructions:

Blend one cup mayonnaise and one cup sour cream in a small bowl. Add 3 tablespoons dip mix; stir until well blended. Chill for 4 hours to blend flavors. Serve with tortilla chips or veggie sticks.

Celebrate a Southwestern-style Christmas by giving bags
of Fiesta Dip Mix in a cowboy hat, wrapped inside
a festive red bandanna.

Wintertime Cereal Mix

Megan Brooks
Antioch, TN

*A warm cereal that tastes wonderful made with
dried cherries, cranberries or blueberries too.*

5 c. instant oats, uncooked
1/4 c. brown sugar, packed

1 c. raisins
3 T. powdered milk

Combine all ingredients in a large bowl. Store in an airtight container
until ready to use. To serve, stir together one cup cereal mix and 1/2 to
3/4 cup boiling water in a cereal bowl. Let stand until thickened.
Makes 10 servings.

Arrange Wintertime Cereal Mix alongside packages of
herbal tea, jars of honey, jam and warm muffins on a vintage
serving tray...just the right gift delivered on a wintry morning!

Berry Scone Mix in a Jar

Brenda Smith
Gooseberry Patch

*To make vanilla sugar…simply slice a vanilla bean in half
lengthwise and add both halves to 1/2 cup sugar.
Let stand for 2 weeks.*

2 c. all-purpose flour	1 t. lemon zest
1/2 c. vanilla sugar	1/4 t. salt
1/4 c. powdered milk	1/3 c. shortening
2 t. baking powder	1 c. sweetened, dried blueberries

Stir together flour, sugar, milk, baking powder, lemon zest and salt
in a large bowl. Cut in shortening using a pastry cutter or fork, until
mixture resembles coarse crumbs. Stir in berries. Pour into a one-quart,
wide-mouth canning jar; pack down gently. Add additional berries
to fill jar if necessary. Secure lid; attach instructions. Store at room
temperature for up to 6 weeks, or freeze up to 6 months.

Instructions:

Place scone mix in a large bowl; toss gently to mix. Add one beaten
egg and 1/4 cup water; stir just until moistened. Turn dough out onto a
lightly floured surface; quickly knead gently for 12 to 15 strokes, or
until nearly smooth. Pat to 1/2-inch thick. Cut into desired shapes and
place one inch apart on an ungreased baking sheet. Brush with milk.
Bake at 400 degrees for 12 to 15 minutes, or until golden. Transfer to
a wire rack to cool slightly; serve warm. Makes 6 to 8 scones.

Good morning! Pair up
Berry Scone Mix in a
jar with a crock of real
butter for a yummy
breakfast-time gift.

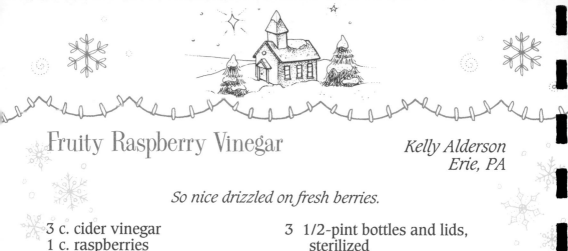

Fruity Raspberry Vinegar

Kelly Alderson
Erie, PA

So nice drizzled on fresh berries.

3 c. cider vinegar
1 c. raspberries
2 T. sugar

3 1/2-pint bottles and lids,
　sterilized

Combine all ingredients in a medium glass mixing bowl; mix gently. Using a funnel, carefully pour mixture into bottles; cover tightly with lids and store at room temperature. Makes 3 bottles.

Rosemary Vinegar

Anna McMaster
Portland, OR

Adds a great flavor to steamed veggies.

4 c. white vinegar
2/3 c. water
6 sprigs fresh rosemary

4 1/2-pint bottles and lids,
　sterilized

Combine vinegar and water in a saucepan over medium-high heat until mixture begins to boil. Remove from heat. Slip 3 sprigs of rosemary into each bottle. Using a funnel, carefully pour the hot vinegar into the bottles. Cover tightly with lids; store at room temperature. Makes 4 bottles.

Salad dressings, sauces and marinades will all get some extra zing with a splash of flavored vinegar. Add some sparkle to the bottle by threading several beads onto lengths of 16-gauge wire. Using pliers, curl the end of the wire to keep the beads on, and then wrap each length around the bottle neck.

Hot Pepper Ringers

Connie Bryant
Topeka, KS

*Different from ordinary canned peppers...these
ringers are a special treat!*

1-1/2 lbs. banana peppers, cut
    into one-inch squares
1 lb. jalapeño peppers, cut into
    one-inch squares
1/4 lb. serrano peppers, cut into
    one-inch squares

6 c. vinegar
2 c. water
3 cloves garlic, crushed
5 1-pint canning jars and lids,
    sterilized

Toss peppers together; set aside. Combine vinegar, water and garlic
in a large stockpot; bring to a boil over medium heat. Simmer for
5 minutes; discard garlic. Pack peppers into hot sterilized jars; ladle hot
liquid over peppers, leaving 1/2-inch headspace. Wipe rims; secure
lids. Process in a boiling water bath for 10 minutes; set jars on a towel
to cool. Check for seals. Makes 5 jars.

Surprise a favorite gardener with a jar of Hot Pepper Ringers
delivered in a gathering basket. Tuck in a pocket-size gardening
journal and some seed packets...delightful!

Farmhouse Cookies

Maria Hunt
Waddington, NY

I have great memories of baking these cookies with my grandmother every year. I don't know exactly where the recipe came from, but these cookies were what she was known for.

1 c. butter, softened
2 c. sugar
2 eggs
1 c. sour cream
1 t. vanilla extract

4-1/2 c. all-purpose flour
1/2 t. baking soda
4 t. baking powder
Optional: 3/4 c. chopped nuts,
    1/2 c. raisins

Blend together butter and sugar in a large bowl; add eggs, one at a time. Beat in sour cream and vanilla; set aside. Combine flour, baking soda and baking powder in a separate bowl; blend thoroughly. Gradually add flour mixture into butter mixture; mix well. Dough should be fairly thick. Roll out on a floured surface. Using a large cookie cutter, cut out cookies and arrange on an ungreased baking sheet. Sprinkle with nuts and raisins, if desired. Bake at 350 degrees for 15 to 18 minutes. Makes about 2 to 3 dozen.

Edge a colorful paper plate with pinking shears and top with sheets of tissue paper. Arrange a selection of cookies on top and then slide the plate into a cellophane bag. Tied up with a red gingham ribbon, it makes a simply yummy gift!

Double Peanut Butter Cookies

Shari Miller
Hobart, IN

*In the late 1960's, when I was in the first grade, I got an Easy Bake
Oven for Christmas...I was so excited! My friend and neighbor, Joe,
would come over and for hours on end we would bake and bake.
Years later, after we had outgrown the oven, Mom had a yard sale...in
it was my oven, just waiting for another little girl to have and enjoy.*

1-1/2 c. all-purpose flour	1/2 c. shortening
1/2 c. sugar	1/2 c. creamy peanut butter
1/2 t. baking soda	1/4 c. light corn syrup
1/4 t. salt	1 T. milk

Combine flour, sugar, baking soda and salt. Blend in shortening
and peanut butter until mixture resembles coarse meal. Blend in
syrup and milk. Form into a roll 2 inches thick; chill. Slice 1/8-inch
to 1/4-inch thick. Arrange half the slices on ungreased baking sheets;
spread each with 1/2 teaspoon peanut butter. Top with remaining
slices; seal edges with a fork. Bake at 350 degrees for 12 minutes,
or until golden. Makes 2 dozen.

A mini mailbox of goodies makes a terrific treat for a far-away
friend. Fill the mailbox with packets of candy-striped stationery
and envelopes, stamps, cookies, candies and gift mixes. Tuck in
a phone card so you can catch up on holiday plans!

Peppermint Stick Treats

Denise Mainville
Huber Heights, OH

Great for stocking stuffers or to simply say happy holidays to family & friends!

2 1-oz. sqs. semi-sweet baking   1/3 c. chopped walnuts
   chocolate, chopped   8 4-inch peppermint sticks
1 t. shortening

Combine chocolate and shortening in a small saucepan over low heat; stir until melted. Transfer to a bowl. Spread chopped nuts on wax paper. Dip one end of peppermint sticks into chocolate; roll in nuts. Place on wax paper and let stand until set. Wrap each stick in a clear plastic bag and tie at end. Makes 8.

Look for vellum bags at craft stores...they turn simple treats into the sweetest gifts! Fill bags with Peppermint Stick Treats, fold over the top and seal closed with a sticker.

Coal Candy

Wendy Jacobs
Idaho Falls, ID

A fun little reminder to be nice and not naughty!

2 c. sugar
2/3 c. light corn syrup
3/4 c. water

1 to 2 t. black food coloring
   paste
1 t. anise flavoring oil

In a heavy saucepan, mix together sugar, corn syrup and water; stir over medium heat until sugar dissolves. Bring mixture to a boil without stirring. Wash down any sugar crystals that form on the sides of the pan with a wet pastry brush. Continue to cook syrup until a candy thermometer reaches 260 degrees; add coloring. Continue to boil without stirring until thermometer reaches exactly 300 degrees. Remove from heat when finished boiling; add flavoring. Pour syrup into a lightly greased 8"x8" baking pan; cool completely at room temperature. Using a wooden spoon, break candy into coal-like pieces. Wrap candy in small plastic bags and secure with twist ties. Makes 4 to 5 dozen pieces.

Coal Candy tucked inside Christmas stockings is sure
to bring lots of laughs Christmas morning!

Warm & Spicy Cranberry Cider Mix

Mary Murray
Gooseberry Patch

It's so nice to put your feet up by the fire and enjoy a cup of warm cider on a chilly winter night.

1/2 c. sweetened, dried
   cranberries
12 4-inch cinnamon sticks

1/2 t. whole cloves, crushed
2 T. whole allspice

Combine all ingredients together; store in an airtight container. Attach instructions.

Instructions:

Combine 2 quarts cider, one quart water and contents of cranberry cider mix. Heat through without boiling; add one sliced orange. Serve warm; garnish with additional orange slices, if desired. Serves 12 to 14.

For a real winter warmer, give packets of Warm & Spicy Cranberry Cider Mix tucked down inside a thermos.

Orange-Cinnamon Tea Mix

Claire Bertram
Lexington, KY

Red cinnamon candies give this a punch of flavor.

18-oz. jar orange drink mix	1/3 c. instant tea mix
2 c. sugar	1 t. ground cinnamon
1/2 c. red cinnamon candies	1 t. ground cloves

Combine all ingredients; store in an airtight container. Attach instructions. Makes 5 cups mix.

Instructions:

To serve, stir 1-1/2 tablespoons of tea mix into one cup hot water, stirring until candies dissolve.

Slip a plastic zipping bag of Orange-Cinnamon Tea Mix into a pretty teapot. Tuck in a dainty silver spoon and tie on a gift tag...so sweet.

Peppermint Candy Canes

*Diana Chaney
Olathe, KS*

An old-fashioned recipe that's sure to bring smiles!

2 c. sugar
1/2 c. light corn syrup
1/2 c. water

1/4 t. cream of tartar
3/4 t. peppermint extract
3/4 to 1 t. red food coloring

In a large, heavy saucepan, blend together sugar, corn syrup, water and cream of tartar; stir to dissolve sugar. Cook over medium heat until candy thermometer reaches the hard-ball stage, or 250 to 269 degrees on a candy thermometer. Remove from heat. Add peppermint extract; blend well. Divide into 2 portions. Add coloring to one portion; mix well. Pour candy onto 2 greased plates; let cool. When cool enough to handle, form into 2 ropes; twist white and red candy together. Cut into desired lengths and form into canes. Makes 6.

Wrap individual Peppermint Candy Canes in colorful plastic wrap...just right for sharing with co-workers.

Stained Glass Candy

Samantha Sparks
Madison, WI

*You can use any flavor of extract or color of
food coloring in this easy recipe.*

1 c. water
3-1/2 c. sugar
1-1/2 c. light corn syrup

1 T. almond extract
1 T. red food coloring

Combine water, sugar and corn syrup in a large heavy saucepan over
medium-high heat, stirring constantly. When sugar dissolves, bring
to a boil without stirring, until mixture reaches the hard-crack stage,
or 290 to 310 degrees on a candy thermometer. Remove from heat.
When mixture stops bubbling, stir in extract and coloring. Spread
1/4-inch thick in a greased 18"x12" jelly-roll pan. Cool for 45 minutes
in refrigerator. Break into pieces. Makes 2-1/2 dozen.

Stained Glass Candy is so pretty...give it in a clear glass canning
or apothecary jar topped off with a bow.

Orangy-Ginger Biscotti

Carrie O'Shea
Marina Del Ray, CA

The flavor of this biscotti will keep you coming back for more!

2/3 c. almonds
1-3/4 c. cake flour
2 t. ground ginger
1 t. baking powder
1 c. butter, softened
1 c. brown sugar, packed

6 T. plus 2 t. sugar
2 T. orange zest
2 egg yolks, divided and beaten
1/2 t. vanilla extract
2/3 c. pistachios, chopped

Finely grind almonds, flour, ginger and baking powder in a food processor; set aside. Blend together butter, brown sugar and 6 tablespoons sugar until light and fluffy. Add zest, one egg yolk and vanilla; beat well. Mix in dry ingredients; stir just until blended. Stir in pistachios. Divide dough in half. Using floured hands, roll each half on a lightly floured surface into a 1/2-inch thick log. Arrange logs 4 inches apart on a greased and floured baking sheet. Cover with plastic wrap; refrigerate for one hour. Brush logs with remaining egg yolk; sprinkle with remaining sugar. Bake at 350 degrees for about 30 minutes, until deep golden and firm to touch. Let cool for 10 minutes. Using a serrated knife, cut logs crosswise into 1/2-inch thick slices. Arrange sliced-side down on baking sheet. Bake at 300 degrees until golden on top, about 12 minutes. Turn over; bake until golden, about 12 minutes. Transfer biscotti to a wire rack; cool completely. Store in an airtight container at room temperature. Makes 1-1/2 dozen.

Deliver Orangy-Ginger Biscotti
wrapped up in a tea towel
inside a new paint can...an ideal
holiday housewarming gift!

Creamy Cranberry Cookie Mix

Jen Eveland-Kupp
Blandon, PA

Tangy cranberries mixed with white chocolate...scrumptious!

1 c. all-purpose flour
1/2 t. baking soda
1/2 t. salt
1/3 c. sugar
1/2 c. quick-cooking oats, uncooked

1/3 c. brown sugar, packed
1/2 c. sweetened dried cranberries
1/2 c. white chocolate chips
1/2 c. chopped pecans

Combine flour, baking soda and salt; pour into a one-quart, wide-mouth canning jar. Pack firmly; add sugar, packing down again. Layer remaining ingredients in order listed; pack firmly after each layer. Secure lid and attach instructions.

Instructions:

Pour cookie mix into a large bowl; stir to mix. In a separate bowl, blend together 1/2 cup softened butter, one egg and one teaspoon vanilla extract until fluffy. Gradually add dry ingredients; mix with an electric mixer on low speed or a wooden spoon until well blended. Drop by heaping teaspoonfuls onto greased baking sheets. Bake at 350 degrees for 8 to 10 minutes until lightly golden. Let cool for 5 minutes; remove to wire rack. Makes 1-1/2 dozen.

Baking fun, with no fuss! Place a jar of Creamy Cranberry Cookie Mix on a new baking sheet. Tie it all up with wide ribbon, then slip a wooden spoon through the bow. A busy mom will love it!

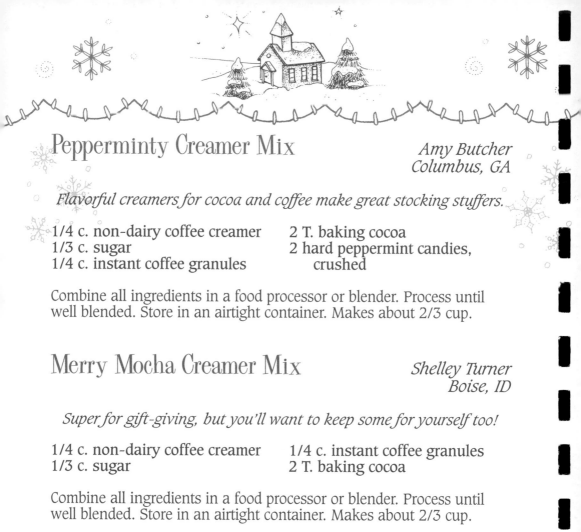

Pepperminty Creamer Mix

Amy Butcher
Columbus, GA

Flavorful creamers for cocoa and coffee make great stocking stuffers.

1/4 c. non-dairy coffee creamer
1/3 c. sugar
1/4 c. instant coffee granules

2 T. baking cocoa
2 hard peppermint candies,
   crushed

Combine all ingredients in a food processor or blender. Process until well blended. Store in an airtight container. Makes about 2/3 cup.

Merry Mocha Creamer Mix

Shelley Turner
Boise, ID

Super for gift-giving, but you'll want to keep some for yourself too!

1/4 c. non-dairy coffee creamer
1/3 c. sugar

1/4 c. instant coffee granules
2 T. baking cocoa

Combine all ingredients in a food processor or blender. Process until well blended. Store in an airtight container. Makes about 2/3 cup.

Fill milk bottles with Merry Mocha and Pepperminty
Creamer Mixes, then create gift tags using a vintage photo.

Ice Cream Bread

Kim Conner
South Boston, VA

*I like to top slices of this simple bread with jelly or jam.
Remember not to use low-fat ice cream in this recipe.*

1 pint ice cream, softened   1-1/2 c. self-rising flour

Mix together ice cream and flour. Pour into a greased and floured
7"x3" loaf pan; bake at 350 degrees for 40 to 45 minutes. Makes
one loaf.

Plum Jam

Sharon Tillman
Hampton, VA

*A jar of homemade jam adds so much to a gift of bread,
muffins or scones.*

4 lbs. plums, pitted and chopped   1/4 c. lemon juice
6 c. sugar   4 1-pint jars with lids, sterilized
1-1/2 c. water

Combine all ingredients in a saucepan; bring to a boil over medium
heat, stirring occasionally until sugar dissolves. Cook rapidly until
mixtures coats the back of a spoon, about 20 minutes. As mixture
thickens, stir frequently to prevent sticking. Pour into hot sterilized
jars, leaving 1/4-inch headspace. Wipe rims; secure lids with rings.
Process in a boiling water bath for 10 to 15 minutes. Cool on a towel;
check for seals. Makes 4 jars.

For individual treats, stack 3 or 4 slices of Ice Cream Bread,
wrap in wax paper and tie up with bright red rick rack.

Chestnut Truffles

Sharon Demers
Dolores, CO

This can be made up to 5 days in advance. Do not roll truffles in powdered sugar mixture until ready to serve.

1/2 c. whipping cream
8-oz. pkg. semi-sweet baking
    chocolate, chopped
2 T. dark corn syrup
12 chestnuts packed in syrup,
    drained, patted dry and
    coarsely chopped

1/4 c. powdered sugar
1/4 c. baking cocoa

Bring whipping cream to a simmer in a small saucepan over medium heat. Remove from stove; stir in chocolate and corn syrup, stirring until chocolate is melted. Fold in chestnuts; transfer to a medium bowl. Refrigerate for one hour. Scoop out mixture by 2 teaspoonfuls and form into balls; place on parchment-lined baking sheets. Refrigerate until firm, 15 to 30 minutes. Combine sugar and cocoa in a shallow bowl; roll truffles in mixture, coating completely. Store in an airtight container in refrigerator or a cool, dry place until ready to serve. Makes about 2 dozen.

Fill a colorful paper cone with Chestnut Truffles,
add a ribbon hanger and loop over the doorknob of
a best friend...she'll love them!

Buckeye Bars

Dawn Myers
Springfield, OH

An Ohio all-time favorite treat!

1 c. margarine
1-1/2 c. creamy peanut butter,
   divided

16-oz. pkg. powdered sugar
8-oz. pkg. milk chocolate
   candy bar, broken up

Melt together margarine and one cup peanut butter in a microwave-safe bowl on high setting for about 1-1/2 minutes. Mix well. Stir in powdered sugar; pat into a lightly greased 13"x9" baking pan. Melt together chocolate and remaining peanut butter in a microwave-safe bowl on high setting for about 1-1/2 minutes; stir until well blended. Pour chocolate mixture over peanut butter mixture. Chill in refrigerator until firm; cut into squares. Makes about 5 dozen.

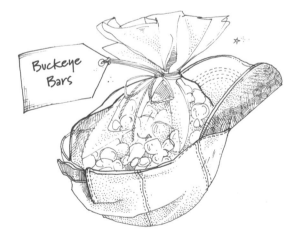

Football fans will cheer when they find Buckeye Bars
slipped inside a new ball cap. Don't forget to add a pair
of tickets to the big game!

Gifts for Giving...
festive wrapping ideas!

Search flea markets for old-fashioned milk bottles...
just right for filling with bite-size candies.

A regular, quart-size Mason jar
filled with peppermint candies,
gumdrops or chocolates easily
becomes a whimsical candle jar.
Just set an oyster jar votive holder
inside the jar rim and add a
votive candle to the holder.

Top jars of layered cookie mixes with a
charming handkerchief.

Arrange mini cupcakes inside a vintage cake mold.

Slip an herb dip mix inside a mini watering can.

Layer slices of fruity quick bread in berry
baskets...top with a rick rack bow.

Line a vintage pail with a tea towel
and tuck fudge squares or peanut
clusters inside.

Nestle bags of herbal tea inside
a sweet little teapot.

The Tradition of the Tin Cup

Our family had always read the story of "Laura's Best Christmas Ever" from the *Little House on the Prairie* series of books. I had always hoped it would instill in our daughter, Carrie, how thankful we should be for all of the many blessings we had, even if we didn't receive all of the things we had hoped for on Christmas morning. It was often hard to imagine that Laura's best Christmas consisted of 2 peppermint sticks, a heart-shaped cake, an orange and a penny tucked inside a brand new tin cup of her very own.

As the years passed and Carrie reached middle-school age, her wish list was more extensive and definitely more expensive. One year she was called into the family room on Christmas Eve and was told that there was a surprise for her. She gingerly walked down the hall and was taken back for a moment...her eyes twinkled at the sight of the tree, but there weren't any boxes underneath it. Then she smiled at the sight on the mantel...2 peppermint sticks, a heart-shaped cake, an orange and a penny tucked inside a brand-new tin cup. She read the story and truly realized that just in case she didn't receive all of the things on her list, she should be happy with what she did receive.

The tradition continued through her college years and as she became a newlywed. Ten years have passed and I have received many gifts, including 2 precious grandchildren. It's nice to know the tradition of the tin cup and what it represents will carry on through another generation.

Deborah Coberly-Goranflo
La Grange, KY

One Special Christmas

One Christmas morning when my 4 children were still at home, we woke up to find that our electricity had gone off during the night due to a storm. As we all began to gather in the living room, we became disappointed that our plans of cooking Christmas dinner had been ruined...or so we thought.

As we were sitting together, we decided to build a fire to keep warm and then as we all gathered by the fire, we began talking. We talked about conveniences of the modern day and the differences of that first Christmas morning. We talked about the commercial side of Christmas and the true meaning of Christmas. About that time, the electricity came back on and our quiet atmosphere was interrupted. Suddenly, one of the kids jumped up and turned out all the lights. We continued our time together of sharing and thankfulness. It turned out to be one of the most memorable Christmases ever. Now a Christmas doesn't go by that we don't talk about that morning, when the true meaning of Christmas became so real to us.

Charlotte Loupe
Beaumont, TX

A New Stocking

Ever since I can remember, on Christmas morning we always received a stocking with an apple, an orange and nuts along with presents from Santa. When I was 16 years old and putting together a stocking for my mother, I couldn't find her Christmas stocking. To improvise, I opened a pair of pantyhose and put an apple in one foot, an orange in the other and scattered nuts and candy into the legs, then placed a big present at the top. Needless to say, she was surprised and also got a great laugh out of it!

Jennifer Breeden
Chesterfield, VA

The Christmas Star

The Christmas memory I love most is my sister and I taking turns putting the star on the tree. This was a tradition that we looked forward to every year, and now that I have children, we let them take turns putting the star on. I see the same excitement each year in their eyes that I had in mine as a child.

Kim Hartless
Forest, VA

Surprises

My youngest daughter, Michelle, loved to shake the gifts under the tree and prided herself on being able to guess almost every gift before she opened it. One year, in an attempt to make her surprises more special, I decided to wrap up some noisemakers and a rock along with some paper money in a large box. It was so much fun watching her open the box to find something she didn't expect! We still remember this every season and all the fun it brought to Michelle and our family.

Linda Marcinowski
Alexandria, VA

A Note from Santa

When we had a fireplace insert added to our fireplace in the family room, our son worried about how Santa would get into our house to bring his toys. He would open the door to the insert, shake his head and say, "Never gonna happen, no way, no how."

So, on Christmas Eve that year, he finally came to me and asked how I thought Santa would get himself and the toys down the chimney. I reassured him that I was sure Santa would be able to use the same magic to get in through the insert. He was still shaking his head as he was going to bed.

I always got up first on Christmas morning to make sure the tree was lit and my camera was ready, but this year was a little different. I stopped in my tracks as I walked into the family room…the fireplace insert door was open, there were ashes on the carpet and not only Santa's footprints, but reindeer ones as well. When my son walked in, he noticed a note on the Christmas tree. It read:

Dear Ronnie, Jr.

Never doubt what I can do, for through my love for you, I would never let you down. The fireplace insert was really tight, then I felt a tap on my shoulder and it was Rudolph always lending that extra bit that I need. So he helped me push and we tumbled. Please tell Mom I'm sorry about the mess. Merry Christmas, and remember to say your prayers and love all mankind.

Santa

Ellana Deen
Charlotte, NC

Sweet Holiday
MEMORIES

The Red Snowsuit

Being a Michigan girl, I had to wear my one-piece red snowsuit every time I went outside in the winter. I remember how much I hated to get into that suit back in 1962 when I was 5 years old.

Now, I love looking back at the pictures Mom has of me wearing that suit. There is a picture of me giving my beloved pony, Dolly, big hoop earrings, because that is what Dolly "asked" Santa for Christmas. When I see that particular picture I get all warm and fuzzy inside. I loved my red snowsuit and my pony, Dolly.

Elizabeth Powers
Rochester Hills, MI

Waiting to See Santa

When I was little, Dad would take me and my sisters to a local store to see Santa arrive in a helicopter on Thanksgiving Day. The parking lot would be roped off and the kids would line up to wait for Santa to land. Every year when the helicopter came, all the kids would cheer and wave at Santa, then he would run around the parking lot shaking sleigh bells and shouting, "Ho, ho, ho!"

The staff at the store had a path roped off for all the kids to visit Santa and we all received a button that said, "I visited Santa at Throckmorton's." This is a memory I will keep in my heart forever and I love my Dad, Mom and sisters for making it!

Dusty Huff
Huber Heights, OH

Sweet Holiday
MEMORIES

The Train Around the Tree

One of my favorite Christmas memories is of Dad and me setting up our Lionel train set every year around the Christmas tree. A few days before Christmas, Dad would bring down all the boxes from the attic and we would get to work setting up the track and building our village. Then, when everything was set up just right, we would put on our conductors' hats and watch the train go around and around. My husband and I are now continuing this tradition with our son and I hope the memories of this wonderful time will stay with him as they did with me.

Diane Wehrenberg
Hopatcong, NJ

Memory Book

Each year starting December 1st, we have a memory book that we set out for family and guests who come to our home during the holidays. They write about anything they would like...the weather, births, graduations and family events. We've found it's a great way to keep track of all that's happened throughout the year. Even the little ones add to the book...a chocolate handprint or an outline of their foot or hand is so sweet.

Patty Moyer
Milan, OH

A Family Christmas

During the holidays, I remember the excitement of Christmas shopping at the 5 & dime store and of our family gathered around the piano. We weren't the best singers, but it gave us all that special feeling of family. Getting up on Christmas morning with the wood stove roaring, the smell of popcorn balls and of course the tree and presents...Mom really made Christmas special.

Brenda Degreenia
Barre, VT

Sweet Holiday
MEMORIES

All Together for the Holidays

The day after Thanksgiving, all my grandchildren and I take a train to Philadelphia to see the light show at Lord & Taylor, then we go to Strawbridge to see the Dickens village. We enjoy lunch together and return home on the train. When my children and grandchildren arrive on Christmas Eve, they'll find stockings hung on the stair steps waiting for each of them. The stockings are filled with new slippers and pajamas and as soon as everyone has changed, we take family photos. I have 9 grandchildren and 4 children and spouses...we truly enjoy Christmas together as family.

Eileen Yost
Hatboro, PA

Camping Under the Tree

My husband, 2 children and I always get our Christmas tree from a tree farm. It may take us awhile, but we walk around until we find just the right tree. Once we find it, we always stop for hot cocoa on the way home. Then, when Christmas vacation starts for the kids, we take one night and camp out on the floor in front of the tree. We have our hot cocoa and read to them from a Christmas story book that my mother used to read to my sisters and brother and me when we were small.

When Christmas Eve arrives, my parents come and spend the night with us. The best thing of all is that when I think I'm not doing enough as a mom to make their holidays memorable, they tell me that they don't ever want any of it to change, no matter how old they get.

Nikki Canterbury
Cross Lanes, WV

Sweet Holiday
MEMORIES

Vacation Photos

Every year we make our vacations special by visiting a different location. We take our favorite family photo from that summer vacation and turn it into our annual Christmas card. Whether we were standing on the rocks in Sedona, Arizona, walking on the coast in Maine or hiking in Kentucky, there's no need for a lengthy holiday letter…a picture does speak a thousand words.

Mary Bloom
Nazareth, PA

A Christmas Picnic

My family loves putting up the tree at Christmas. The night we put up our decorations, our family has a picnic dinner under the Christmas tree. We turn down the lights and just leave the tree lights twinkling, spread out a blanket and feast on sandwiches, chips and other picnic goodies. Then Mom hands out our new ornaments for the year. What Christmas fun!

Erin Murphy
Evanston, IL

Reindeer Food

I have a very special bond with my great-niece, and ever since she was 2 years old we've been making a big batch of reindeer food. We simply pour oats into a container, add chopped nuts and a pinch of glitter; shake and sprinkle on the lawn for Santa's reindeer. My niece looks forward to this ritual every year. It's been a great way to show children that we believe in things we can't always see, and to have faith and hope in everything that we do.

Michelle Eva Papp
Rutherford, NJ

Pictures by the Tree

There wasn't a Christmas that Grandpa June, my dad, didn't take a picture of the grandkids under the tree. It all started with their first Christmas in the infant seat on the floor. As the years passed, the kids grew and the tree looked smaller and smaller. It's been such fun to look back and see how the kids have changed over the years. I now have a granddaughter and I follow Dad's tradition…Ava had her picture taken in her car seat in front of the tree!

Cheri Stees
Lena, IL

Sweet Holiday
MEMORIES

Holiday Traditions

We have a favorite tradition on Christmas Eve that makes the evening feel magical. We begin with dinner, which is always served fondue-style. I love this because it doesn't take much time to prepare, and gives me more time with my family. We then go to our Christmas Eve candlelight and communion service. After church, we take the long way home to look at the Christmas lights.

Once we're home, we open gifts from all of our out-of-town friends & family. Not only does this help make it easier to wait for Christmas morning, but it also helps clear out from under the tree for Santa's visit! Christmas is such a magical time, it makes me feel so warm and loved.

Kristi Kavicky
Collierville, TN

Gifts from Mrs. Claus

In May of 1964 my dad passed away and left behind my mom and 6 small children. That Christmas all of us came down with chickenpox and we had to stay at home with no visitors allowed. On Christmas Eve, we had a big snowstorm, but somehow, a delivery truck from a local department store made its way to our farmhouse. Mom answered the door and the delivery man came in bearing gifts for everyone! Mom asked them who the presents were from, and the response was "They came from Mrs. Claus." For years we tried to find out who "Mrs. Claus" was, but we still have no idea.

About 10 years ago, our local newspaper was running a request for readers to submit their most memorable Christmas stories and I submitted mine. It was published, and a week after the paper went out, I received a letter from the newspaper office. They were asked to forward it on to me because the sender wanted to remain secret. The letter was from "Mrs. Claus." She gave me a few details about that Christmas in 1964, and she explained how she had wanted to help our family. Christmas is a special time for me and my family, and I know the true meaning of Christmas because of that wonderful person who calls herself "Mrs. Claus." I am eternally grateful for the joy she brought to me as a 5-year-old child in 1964.

Marie Wagner
Manitowoc, WI

Sweet Holiday
MEMORIES

Santa's Coming!

I have a special Christmas memory that I have always treasured. One time when I was little, I heard the sound of sleigh bells, prancing hooves and Santa's voice coming down the chimney. My parents had always told my siblings and me that if Santa ever came and we were awake, he would leave and try to come back later. Well, we were so afraid our Christmas wishes wouldn't come true, that we ran upstairs and buried our heads in our pillows trying to fall asleep! Later on, we found out that our parents had recorded the tape and placed it inside the chimney. They had wanted us to get to bed and boy did we! What a neat memory. I now have children of my own and hope that my husband and I can create those kinds of precious memories for our children.

Michelle Melton
Tyler, TX

The Advent Calendar

The first year my husband and I were married, he created an advent calendar for me filled with wonderful notes and trinkets. We had so much fun with it, that we decided to alternate which one of us created the calendar and which one of us received it. One year, I came up with a fortune cookie theme for our calendar. I found a company that created custom fortune cookies and I made a list of 24 family sayings for the fortunes. With a fortune cookie and a trinket in each of 24 Chinese take-out cartons, we had a blast opening one container each evening, laughing over what was inside. We have had many unique advent calendars over the years, but this one will be remembered as a real highlight!

Susan Brown
Seattle, WA

Sweet Holiday
MEMORIES

Gingerbread House Building

Each year at Christmas, since my sons were young, I have baked a gingerbread house. The decorating part is a family event and so we set aside one night to assemble and decorate the house. The kitchen table is loaded down with a variety of candy, chocolates, sugar cubes and decorations. We've learned that the more icing we use, the sturdier the house is and so far it has never collapsed!

My sons are now 18 and 13 years old and around Thanksgiving they began asking what night is set aside for decorating our gingerbread house. I'm not sure which I enjoy more...the family fun building the house, or the sight of all the neighborhood children coming in for the demolition and eating. Both are precious memories that I hope will carry on to the next generation.

Elaine Pettit
Clearwater, FL

The Bear Sweater

I nicknamed my son Bear when he was very young, and over the years he's made a point of buying bear-themed cards for Mothers' Day and my birthday. Each Christmas, there was also a new little bear waiting for me. One year, when I came downstairs Christmas morning, there was no bear. At first I felt a little twinge of disappointment, but reasoned that, at his age, he probably felt it was too childish a tradition to continue. As we settled down to hand out gifts, he handed me a package and watched intently as I unwrapped it, all the while saying, "If it's not right, you can return it." "It" turned out to be a beautiful red Christmas sweater sporting the fluffiest white polar bears! "Did you see? It has bears. I thought you could wear it today." And wear it I did…it was 2 sizes too small, but it was cotton, and later as I was dressing, that sweater lost a stretching tug-of-war. As I sat down to Christmas dinner that day in my beautiful sweater, my son asked again, "You really like it? It's all right?" I answered, "It's more than all right, it's absolutely perfect." And it was.

Peggy Donnally
Toledo, OH

218

Christmas Countdown

I know my love of Christmas stems from the many wonderful memories I have growing up in the small town of Northampton, Pennsylvania. During our childhood, my mom would help my brother and me create a Christmas countdown chain which we could hang on our bedposts and then faithfully remove a link each night until the last magical night. On December 6th, St. Nick always paid us a visit and left apples, oranges, nuts, a gingerbread man and a small toy. Around this time, we would eagerly help Dad in putting up the Christmas decorations, complete with trains, houses, trees and people ice skating on a little lake. It seemed waiting another year was so long until we could once again repeat our ever-anticipated traditions.

Kristin Berke
Walnutport, PA

INDEX

INDEX

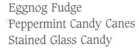

INDEX

We've cooked up a whole collection of Gooseberry Patch® books!

Have a taste for more? Call us toll-free at
1-800-854-6673
We'll send you our latest catalog filled with kitchenware, candles, handmade quilts, gourmet goodies, enamelware, bowls, night lights and our very own line of cookbooks, calendars and organizers!

Phone us:
1·800·854·6673

Fax us:
1·740·363·7225

Visit our website:
www.gooseberrypatch.com

Send us your favorite recipe!

*and the memory that makes it special for you!** If we select your recipe for a brand-new **Gooseberry Patch** cookbook, your name will appear right along with it...and you'll receive a FREE copy of the book! Mail to:

Gooseberry Patch
Attn: Book Dept.
P.O. Box 190
Delaware, OH 43015

*Please include the number of servings and all other necessary information!

sparkling snowflakes   rosy cheeks

warm gingerbread

chocolatey cocoa

fresh-cut pine

crackling fires   frosty windowpanes   sleigh bells

U.S. to Canadian recipe equivalents

Volume Measurements

1/4 teaspoon	1 mL
1/2 teaspoon	2 mL
1 teaspoon	5 mL
1 tablespoon = 3 teaspoons	15 mL
2 tablespoons = 1 fluid ounce	30 mL
1/4 cup	60 mL
1/3 cup	75 mL
1/2 cup = 4 fluid ounces	125 mL
1 cup = 8 fluid ounces	250 mL
2 cups = 1 pint =16 fluid ounces	500 mL
4 cups = 1 quart	1 L

Weights

1 ounce	30 g
4 ounces	120 g
8 ounces	225 g
16 ounces = 1 pound	450 g

Oven Temperatures

300° F	150° C
325° F	160° C
350° F	180° C
375° F	190° C
400° F	200° C
450° F	230° C

Baking Pan Sizes

Square

8x8x2 inches	2 L = 20x20x5 cm
9x9x2 inches	2.5 L = 23x23x5 cm

Rectangular

13x9x2 inches	3.5 L = 33x23x5 cm

Loaf

9x5x3 inches	2 L = 23x13x7 cm

Round

8x1-1/2 inches	1.2 L = 20x4 cm
9x1-1/2 inches	1.5 L = 23x4 cm